Practicing Intellectual Freedom in Libraries

Practicing Intellectual Freedom in Libraries

Shannon M. Oltmann

LIBRARIES UNLIMITED®
An Imprint of ABC-CLIO, LLC
Santa Barbara, California • Denver, Colorado

Library of Congress Cataloging in Publication Control Number: 2019021551

ISBN: 978-1-4408-6312-7 (paperback)
      978-1-4408-6313-4 (ebook)

23 22 21 20 19   1 2 3 4 5

This book is also available as an eBook.

Libraries Unlimited
An Imprint of ABC-CLIO, LLC

ABC-CLIO, LLC
147 Castilian Drive
Santa Barbara, California 93117
www.abc-clio.com

This book is printed on acid-free paper ∞

Manufactured in the United States of America

This book is dedicated to my lovely wife, Beth,
who helped me believe in myself.

Contents

Acknowledgments

Many people helped with the development of *Practicing Intellectual Freedom in Libraries*. First, I want to thank my wife, Beth, whose steadfast belief in me carried me through times of doubt and writer's block. Her willingness and ability to sit down and plan out the work (over and over again) were incredibly helpful and productive. My family, especially my parents, Melody and Duane, have also always believed in me and encouraged me to stretch my wings. Danya, Mike, and Tony provided support and cheered me on. Jack and Nancy Bair provided enthusiastic support and let me spend many weekends working away at their table. Our dog Oliver was a constant companion and steadfast assistant editor, often napping next to my desk while I worked.

Daniel Callison was the first to suggest I write for Libraries Unlimited (LU), where Jessica Gribble has been a stalwart and supportive editor, helping me fine-tune the book. Emma Bailey at LU and Mary Jo Bolduc at the American Library Association helped ensure that I had the appropriate permissions for quoted passages.

Many friends and colleagues have played a role in the development of these ideas and in the writing process. Since we first found ourselves standing next to each other at a poster session, Emily J.M. Knox and I have collaborated several times; each exchange sharpens my grasp of these concepts and how to apply them. I held semiregular working meetings with Lois Scheidt, who seemed confident that I would be able to finish what seemed, at times, a monumental task. Stacy Kowalczyk always had words of wisdom and encouragement. Friends near and far connected with me via social media to root for the book.

At the University of Kentucky, I've been fortunate to have great colleagues. Several of us women met semiregularly for a writing group, spending a few hours a week together in the university library or at nearby coffee shops. The camaraderie of this group helped sustain me. Colleagues at the School of Information Science and the College of Communication and Information were supportive and celebrated milestones with me. My director, Jeffrey T. Huber, was also helpful along this process. Finally, I can't forget to mention Starbucks #2561, my neighborhood store and my home for writing much of this book. Apologies to anyone I've left out!

Introduction

Intellectual freedom is one of the core values of librarianship and a foundational principle for the profession. It has been enshrined as an important concept since the creation of the Library Bill of Rights in 1939 (American Library Association [ALA], 2006b). This book explores intellectual freedom from many angles and perspectives, enabling us to have a deeper appreciation of the principle and a firmer grasp on how to apply it in our daily librarianship.

In this introduction, we'll explore the definition of intellectual freedom and the importance of practicing intellectual freedom skills. We'll also provide a brief synopsis of each chapter in the rest of the book.

DEFINING INTELLECTUAL FREEDOM

What do we mean by intellectual freedom? We need to start with the foundational definition. The ALA has defined "intellectual freedom" as

> the right of every individual to both seek and receive information from all points of view without restriction. [Intellectual freedom] provides for free access to all expressions of ideas through which any and all sides of a question, cause or movement may be explored. (ALA, 2007, para. 1)

Intellectual freedom is often seen as an opposition to censorship; while censorship tries to *restrict* access to some information, intellectual freedom advocates for *open access* to information. Let's examine the first sentence of this definition in detail.

Breaking down the Definition

Though ALA's definition may seem simple, it has several important components that deserve closer scrutiny. The first part is "the right . . ." From the first words, the ALA is arguing that intellectual freedom is a *right* that people have. It is not a frivolous luxury, but something that people deserve to have. We will see, throughout this book, how intellectual freedom is connected to the right to freedom of speech, enshrined in the First Amendment of the U.S. Constitution. This means that intellectual freedom *is*, in fact, a right.

Next, we can see that this right is for "every individual . . ." This, again, is quite broad. Intellectual freedom is not limited to library patrons, to those who can prove citizenship, to those with the ability to pay for access, to those with the most need for certain information, or any other sort of restriction. On the contrary, intellectual freedom is for *every* individual, regardless of circumstances or need.

Looking at the verbs, we see that intellectual freedom covers the right "to both seek and receive information."[1] Seeking is more active—it connotes looking for or questing for something, being in search of particular information. Receiving, on the other hand, is a bit more passive. It can mean that information is made available and the individual takes it in. There are, of course, many ways to make information available, and libraries often do a great job at utilizing multiple means of enabling information access.

The next component of the definition is "from all points of view . . ." This is a key phrase in the definition of intellectual freedom (as we'll see in the second part of the book, when we apply the concept of intellectual freedom to various scenarios in libraries).

Simply put, libraries and other information organizations should strive to offer access to as many points of view as possible. This means, for example, having books that convey both the Republican and Democratic perspectives—as well as socialist, libertarian, and other political viewpoints. If Christian music is available to check out or listen to, then secular music should be available too, as well as music with roots in other religious systems.

Finally, another important phrase is "without restriction . . ." For the ALA, it is important to provide access to all points of view without putting up barriers to any of those viewpoints. A simple anecdote can illustrate the various forms that barriers can take.

At a well-known religious university, some texts about other religions (e.g., Islam and Buddhism) were being kept behind the reference desk. The librarian who shared this anecdote with me said that he wanted to protect the students from potentially harmful information. Unfortunately, his actions resulted in restrictions to information for the students. They had to request access to the books instead of picking them off the shelf; fear of judgment, intimidation, or embarrassment would likely lead some students to not ask for the books—thus, this simple barrier restricted access. Since the books weren't on the shelves, they also could not be found through browsing.

As we can see, each phrase in the definition of intellectual freedom is an essential component to understand the concept. While the idea of intellectual freedom may be fairly straightforward, applying it in various situations in different types of libraries can become more complex and nuanced. The significance of intellectual freedom for the library profession is hard to overstate; it is a core value (see Chapter 4) and the base for one of the most foundational documents of our profession, the Library Bill of Rights.

Intellectual Freedom and the Library Bill of Rights

Interestingly, the Library Bill of Rights does not explicitly mention "intellectual freedom" in its seven principles. Nonetheless, the concept of intellectual freedom is the bedrock on which the Library Bill of Rights is built. For example, the first principle says,

> Books and other library resources should be provided for the interest, information, and enlightenment of all people of the community the library serves. Materials should not be excluded because of the origin, background, or views of those contributing to their creation. (ALA, 2006b, para. 2)

In the first sentence, we see that intellectual freedom should apply not only to books but to other resources as well. *All* items provided by a library should be available to all patrons—all people in the community that the library serves. Each type of library (e.g., school, public, academic, and special) has its own community that it serves. Within that community of patrons, all should be able to access every resource of the library.

In the same vein, items should not be excluded because of the creators' background or views (see Chapter 8 for a discussion of this in relation to the #MeToo movement). Since intellectual freedom calls for access to "all points of view," this statement makes sense.

The second principle of the Library Bill of Rights states, "Libraries should provide materials and information presenting all points of view on current and historical issues. Materials should not be proscribed or removed because of partisan or doctrinal disapproval" (ALA, 2006b, para. 3). This is a further emphasis on providing access to all points of view, even if we disagree with them.

In the abovementioned anecdote, the librarian disagreed with the precepts of other religions, leading him to restrict access to those books. In contrast, an intellectual freedom stance says that we should provide access *even if* we disagree—some of our patrons may want or need access to that very information. It is *not* the librarian's job to decide which information is useful or appropriate. Instead, it is the librarian's job to provide access to as much information as possible.

The third principle of the Library Bill of Rights states, "Libraries should challenge censorship in the fulfillment of their responsibility to provide information and enlightenment" (ALA, 2006b, para. 4). This statement pits censorship in opposition to librarianship. Simply put, librarians should work to oppose censorship, particularly in their institutions.

In the fourth principle, the ALA argues that "libraries should cooperate with all persons and groups concerned with resisting abridgment of free expression and free access to ideas" (ALA, 2006b, para. 5). This takes intellectual freedom beyond the library doors, stating that we need to resist censorship wherever and whenever it occurs. In fact, the ALA has made several statements about national affairs (e.g., government surveillance and net neutrality) in line with this principle (more information can be found on their website).

There are several other groups that advocate for freedom of speech and access to information, such as the Freedom to Read Foundation, the National Coalition Against Censorship, the Comic Book Legal Defense Fund, the Association of American Publishers, and the Electronic Frontier Foundation; at various times, the ALA has cooperated with each of these to spread its message of intellectual freedom. One achievement of this cooperation has been the Freedom to Read Statement (ALA, 2006a), which has been endorsed by several of these groups as well as other organizations.

The fifth principle of the Library Bill of Rights states, "A person's right to use a library should not be denied or abridged because of origin, age, background, or views" (ALA, 2006b, para. 6). This principle is sometimes the most controversial because some people want to limit minors' access to certain information (for an exploration of this in relation to internet filtering, see Chapter 10). However, the ALA has stood firm on this principle. Age alone is an insufficient reason for restricting access to information.

In the sixth principle, the ALA says that "libraries which make exhibit spaces and meeting rooms available to the public they serve should make such facilities available on an equitable basis, regardless of the beliefs or affiliations of individuals or groups requesting their use" (ALA, 2006b, para. 7). This principle is discussed in detail in Chapter 9.

Finally, the seventh principle of the Library Bill of Rights argues that "all people, regardless of origin, age, background, or views, possess a right to privacy and confidentiality in their library use. Libraries should advocate for, educate about, and protect people's privacy, safeguarding all library use data, including personally identifiable information" (ALA, 2006b, para. 8). Although a detailed examination of privacy and confidentiality is beyond the scope of this book, they are addressed in Chapter 3 in conjunction with the freedom to explore. Simply put, privacy helps enable intellectual freedom, by providing space in which people can explore new ideas and information.

As this examination has shown, the Library Bill of Rights is inextricably bound up with intellectual freedom. In fact, intellectual freedom can be seen as the basis of this important foundational document of librarianship.

PRACTICING INTELLECTUAL FREEDOM

This book discusses how to *practice* intellectual freedom: how to think about, develop, implement, and hone skills to protect and enhance intellectual freedom in your library.

It is useful to think of intellectual freedom as both a mental orientation and a set of skills that you can practice. The mental orientation has to do with always trying to improve or increase information access in your library, being alert for ways that access may be restricted, and trying to provide more open information, to the extent that you can. Grounding this mental orientation in a theoretical and philosophical background is helpful and can strengthen it.

Intellectual freedom is also a set of skills that can be applied in libraries. Because it is a set of skills, it is something that can be practiced—rehearsed and improved upon. Here, athletes can be a useful analogy. They practice repeatedly, often daily, going through the same motions over and over again. In the same way, we can practice intellectual freedom, going through the same actions and growing stronger in our responses.

Research on practice has indicated that extensive practice of a skill can lead to one becoming an expert in that area (Ericsson, Krampe, & Tesch-Romer, 1993). This has been popularized as a 10,000-hour rule: some people claim that practicing for 10,000 hours can make you an expert in nearly any skill (e.g., Gladwell, 2008; Kahneman, 2011).

Other researchers, however, have expressed some skepticism about these claims (Hambrick et al., 2014; this article provides a good overview of the research to date). The so-called 10,000-hour rule is an oversimplification of the research that preceded it. In addition, it seems likely that other factors (e.g., innate talent) play a significant role in developing skills. Nonetheless, practice is an important aspect in developing and honing skills.

This has been tested most often in arenas such as chess, playing music, and sports (e.g., Ward, Hodges, Starkes, & Williams, 2007). Yet it seems reasonable to infer that other skills can be honed through practice as well. This book argues that intellectual freedom is such a skill. This mind-set can be practiced and improved.

You could practice it in several ways. For example, you could develop role-playing exercises with colleagues and other staff members and then study ALA guidelines to see what professional ethics and norms suggest as appropriate behavior in these exercises. You can join state-level and national intellectual freedom committees and discussion groups to learn from one another. Reading this book and other texts and articles about intellectual freedom will also keep your mind sharp and prepared to implement intellectual freedom in your library.

Thinking of intellectual freedom as a *practice* is also useful because it can remind us that no one is perfect in intellectual freedom; we all have areas in which we may struggle, question the ideals from time to time, or wonder how to put them into action. We can improve our practice of intellectual freedom on a daily basis. Thus, this book is designed to inform and shape our practice of intellectual freedom in all types of libraries.

THE BREADTH OF INTELLECTUAL FREEDOM

Some people may think that intellectual freedom is only a concern in public libraries, but that simply isn't true. All types of libraries have intellectual freedom issues.

School libraries often face book challenges when students' parents are concerned about the content of certain books. Academic libraries may have to deal with challenges to their patrons' privacy and confidentiality. Special libraries often struggle with questions about restricting access to a limited patron base. These are just a few examples of the many different types of intellectual freedom issues that libraries face in their daily operations.

How can we address these issues? The ALA has provided a great deal of guidance on specific issues—look for interpretations of the Library Bill of Rights. This book provides further guidance, incorporating specific examples as well as theoretical background.

OVERVIEW OF EACH CHAPTER

Part I of the book conceptualizes intellectual freedom, helping us to think about it in an abstract, deep, and deliberate manner. In Chapter 1, we explore the connections between intellectual freedom, access to information, and freedom of speech. This chapter traces the development of a right to receive or access information through several court cases and demonstrates the importance of libraries to this right.

Chapter 2 takes this exploration even further, analyzing three of the predominant theories of freedom of speech to explain how access to information is central to this core freedom; those theories are the marketplace of ideas, democracy, and individual utility or autonomy. These theories can be used together to bolster support for intellectual freedom.

We take a different tack in Chapter 3, thinking about how intellectual freedom enables the freedom to explore new ideas. Because intellectual freedom facilitates access to a wide diversity of ideas, we can think through and imagine various paths and perspectives freely, without fear of repercussion; this also means that privacy is important to intellectual freedom.

In Chapter 4, we discuss how the core values of librarianship (as articulated by the ALA) interact with and strengthen intellectual freedom. Those values are access, confidentiality or privacy, democracy, diversity, education and lifelong learning, intellectual freedom, the public good, preservation, professionalism, service, and social responsibility. Each of these can be viewed in connection to intellectual freedom.

Chapter 5 reviews how the value of intellectual freedom gets enacted in the daily lives of all types of libraries (public, school, academic, and special). We see that the specific implementation of intellectual freedom may vary, depending on the community of patrons that a library serves, but the core value remains.

Part II examines intellectual freedom in action, looking at how this essential value plays out across various scenarios and duties in librarianship. For example, Chapter 6 discusses how to handle challenges to materials in libraries. This occurs when someone, usually a patron, thinks a library should not include certain material (a book, movie, etc.). These sorts of scenarios are perhaps the most common situations in which the value of intellectual freedom is invoked and challenged in libraries.

Another arena in which intellectual freedom is commonly brought up is collection development and weeding, discussed in Chapter 7. We consider how the basic principle of intellectual freedom can inform and guide collection development in all types of libraries.

In Chapter 8, we consider the #MeToo movement against sexual harassment in relation to literature and intellectual freedom. An intellectual freedom orientation gives us a unique (and sometimes fraught) position on whether we should remove literature in protest of the author's character or behavior.

Chapter 9 explores implications for programs, meeting rooms, and exhibit spaces in libraries. Because these spaces are part of libraries, sometimes the public assumes that the library endorses whatever is presented or included in these spaces—even though libraries assume a position of neutrality and nonendorsement. Understanding this position from an intellectual freedom perspective lends strength to the libraries' stance.

Chapter 10 investigates the arguments around internet filtering in libraries. While we recognize that many people have concerns about the vast quantity of unregulated information available online, an intellectual freedom orientation suggests that filtering won't solve problems and may create additional ones.

In Chapter 11, we examine what intellectual freedom might tell us about fake news and false information. As with internet filtering, the answer— particularly from an intellectual freedom perspective—is not to restrict information. The better answer is information literacy for our patrons.

Chapter 12 takes up the complex issue of law enforcement as viewed through an intellectual freedom lens. Because privacy and confidentiality are so important to protecting intellectual freedom, we must be cautious in sharing patron information with law enforcement. Librarians need to understand the different types of warrants, court orders, and other documentation that law enforcement might present and appropriate responses to each; perhaps the most important lesson of this chapter is to have an attorney on retainer to help address these questions if they arise.

The next chapter, Chapter 13, considers copyright. It begins with a brief overview of copyright and some of the exceptions and limitations most relevant to libraries. Because copyright protections can sometimes limit access to information, it is important that librarians understand the law and how it pertains to their institutions. At the same time, some aspects of copyright law can enhance access, such as the provisions that enable interlibrary loan (ILL).

The final chapter, Chapter 14, briefly reviews some trends that can impact intellectual freedom in the present and the future. These trends—global censorship, the right to be forgotten, trigger or content warnings, threats to net neutrality, platform censorship, and complacency—have the potential to deeply impact how intellectual freedom gets enacted across our libraries.

NOTE

1. In this book, "information" should be understood very broadly. Its exact contours have been debated ad infinitum in library and information science. Here, we mean any and all information or ideas, in whatever form that patrons might want, need, come across, seek, or find.

REFERENCES

American Library Association. (2006a). Freedom to read statement. Retrieved from http://www.ala.org/advocacy/intfreedom/freedomreadstatement. Document ID: aaac95d4-2988-0024-6573-10a5ce6b21b2.

American Library Association. (2006b). Library bill of rights. Retrieved from http://www.ala.org/advocacy/intfreedom/librarybill. Document ID: 669fd6a3-8939-3e54-7577-996a0a3f8952.

American Library Association. (2007). Intellectual freedom and censorship Q&A. Retrieved from http://www.ala.org/advocacy/intfreedom/censorship/faq. Document ID: e8ae9ed7-a469-f0d4-adf0-f2770d2ca8e8.

Ericsson, K. A., Krampe, R. T., & Tesch-Romer, C. (1993). The role of deliberate practice in the acquisition of expert performance. *Psychological Review, 100*(3), 363–406.

Gladwell, M. (2008). *Outliers: The story of success.* New York, NY: Little, Brown, & Co.

Hambrick, D. Z., Oswald, F. L., Altmann, E. M., Meinz, E. J., Gobet, F., & Campitelli, G. (2014). Deliberate practice: Is that all it takes to become an expert? *Intelligence, 45*(1), 34–45.

Kahneman, D. (2011). *Thinking, fast and slow.* New York, NY: Farrar, Straus, & Giroux.

Ward, P., Hodges, N. J., Starkes, J. L., & Williams, A. M. (2007). The road to excellence: Deliberate practice and the development of expertise. *High Ability Studies, 18*(2), 119–153.

PART ONE

Conceptualizing Intellectual Freedom

ONE

Intellectual Freedom and Access to Information

In the United States, support for intellectual freedom originates in the First Amendment of the Constitution, which prohibits Congress from "abridging the freedom of speech" of citizens (U.S. Constitution, First Amendment, p. 17). Throughout the years, court cases have established that "speech" encompasses much more than the written or spoken word; it includes film, music, art, dance, and many forms of expression.[1]

The right to freedom of speech is broad in another way as well: it includes the right to access information. In fact, the right to access information (which librarians call "intellectual freedom") is a core component of the right to freedom of speech. Legally, the right to access information is often called "receiving" information.

This chapter traces the connection between intellectual freedom, freedom of speech, information access, and libraries through several court cases. The legal terminology is not especially important here; instead, the key ideas and principles that emerge from the court cases are important.

Portions of this chapter are reprinted from Shannon M. Oltmann, "Intellectual Freedom and Freedom of Speech: Three Theoretical Perspectives," *The Library Quarterly* 86, no. 2 (April 2016): 153–171.

THE FIRST AMENDMENT RIGHT TO ACCESS INFORMATION

The noted First Amendment scholar Rodney Smolla (2005) wrote, "While we usually think of the First Amendment as empowering speakers to speak, it might well be understood as embracing a concomitant right of listeners to listen, viewers to view, or readers to read" (pp. 2–72). Let's elaborate on this a bit.

It is well known that the First Amendment protects our right to freedom of speech—to say nearly anything, with a few notable exceptions (e.g., obscenity or slander). Smolla (2005) said that we need to realize that the First Amendment protects much more than our speech: it protects our listening, viewing, and reading rights as well. These are all ways of *accessing* information, and they are all protected by the First Amendment.

Essentially, the argument is that freedom of speech is impossible or valueless without the right or ability to access or receive information (Bollinger, 1986; Braddon-Mitchell & West, 2004; Burden, 2000; Emerson, 1970; Jones, 1999; Mart, 2003; Smolla, 1993). Extensive support for this connection can be found in the history of U.S. court cases concerning the First Amendment and citizens' freedom of speech.

COURT CASES ABOUT ACCESS TO INFORMATION

A brief review of relevant court cases will demonstrate the centrality of information access to freedom of speech. One of the earliest cases to address access to information was *Martin v. City of Struthers* (1943). In this case, the city of Struthers had banned door-to-door canvassing and handing out leaflets, but a Jehovah's Witness challenged the law. The person argued that distributing information and people's right to get that information were essential elements of freedom of speech.

The Supreme Court ruled that the law in Struthers was too restrictive, noting that the rule prohibited *sharing* speech as well as *receiving* it. Because some people might want to receive such information, it was unfair to ban all people from receiving it. In other words, receiving information (or having access to information) was protected by the Supreme Court.

Soon after, the court ruled to further protect access to information, in *Thomas v. Collins* (1945). This case centered on whether a business could ban union representatives from speaking to its employees. The Supreme Court ruled that employees had a right to hear a union representative speak, calling access to information "necessarily correlative" to freedom of speech (p. 534). Not only did the employees have a right to discuss whether they wanted to join a union but they also had a right to hear information about unionization.

Griswold v. Connecticut (1965) was about distributing information about birth control. At the time, sharing such information was illegal in Connecticut (and most of the United States), and the executive director of Connecticut's Planned Parenthood was convicted of violating the law. The Supreme Court ruled that married couples[2] had a right to access such information because they had a right to privacy in their home. Although the case centered on a right to privacy, the right to access information was also an important factor.

Four years later, the right to receive obscene material was challenged (*Stanley v. Georgia*, 1969). Prior to this case, creating, distributing, and owning obscene material (which is, according to the law, more offensive than pornography) was illegal. While he was being investigated for gambling, Robert Stanley's home was searched and law enforcement found obscene films. Stanley argued that he had a right to privately view such materials in his own home.

Although the Supreme Court noted that producing and distributing obscene material was illegal, it decided that having such "information" in one's private home was legal. In Justice Thurgood Marshall's opinion, Stanley

> is asserting the right to read or observe what he pleases—the right to satisfy his intellectual and emotional needs in the privacy of his own home. He is asserting the right to be free from state inquiry into the contents of his library. (p. 565)

The unanimous court decision declared, "It is now well established that the Constitution protects the right to receive information and ideas" (p. 564). Mart (2003) noted that "by 1969, the right to receive information had become a fundamental right" (pp. 178–179). This means it was well established in the legal system and had been recognized by the Supreme Court as an important part of the First Amendment.

Another important court case is *Richmond Newspapers, Inc. v. Virginia* (1980). At the time, the state of Virginia allowed judges to determine whether the press and the public could be barred from criminal trials. When a judge banned the press from a murder trial, two newspapers sued for access to the courtroom.

In this case, the Supreme Court held that access to criminal trials was an important way for the public to understand government actions and decisions (and this was important for the public to be able to hold government accountable). Access could be denied only in rare cases with strong justification. The justices noted that access to information (particularly government information) was implicitly guaranteed by the First Amendment (*Richmond Newspapers, Inc. v. Virginia*, 1980).

Board of Education v. Pico (1982) was one of the few Supreme Court cases to deal with access to information in libraries. In this case, a school board decided to remove several books from the school library because the books were allegedly "anti-American, anti-Christian, anti-Semitic, and just plain filthy" (p. 853). The books in question included *Slaughterhouse-Five* by Kurt Vonnegut, *The Naked Ape* by Desmond Morris, *Down These Mean Streets* by Piri Thomas, *Go Ask Alice* (anonymous), *Black Boy* by Richard Wright, *A Hero Ain't Nothin' but a Sandwich* by Alice Childress, and *The Fixer* by Bernard Malamud.

Several people filed suit, claiming that the board did not have the authority to remove books from the school library. The Court concluded that even though school boards have wide latitude in guiding minors, they may *not* remove books from a library simply because the board members disagree with the content of the books. In a 5–4 decision, the Supreme Court stated that the right to access information was "an inherent corollary of the rights of free speech" (p. 912).

As these court cases demonstrate, the right to access information is inextricably bound up as part of freedom of speech. Blitz (2006) concluded that "it is now well established that the First Amendment protects not only the rights of people to engage in speech but also the right of audiences to receive it" (p. 800). Receiving information is essentially the same as being able to access it.

WHAT IS A "COROLLARY" OF THE FIRST AMENDMENT?

When we say that access to information is a "corollary" of the First Amendment, we mean that it is a necessary part of freedom of speech— that it *flows logically* from our understanding of the First Amendment. In other words, because the First Amendment protects freedom of speech, it also protects access to information. These two concepts are logically bound together. The U.S. courts have found the right to access to be a corollary of the First Amendment for two reasons.

First, the right to receive ideas and information follows naturally from the speaker's right to disseminate them; without someone to receive (or access) the ideas, the right of free speech is incomparably diminished

(*Lamont v. Postmaster General*, 1965). Imagine speaking in a bare room with no recording device and no one present; that speech would be ephemeral and empty. It would be less powerful and meaningful than one given in front of others or shared with others, where your ideas have the chance to be heard, to be considered, and to become part of the public conversation. For many people, the whole point of speech—of any expression—is to communicate with others.

Second, the right to receive information is "a necessary predicate to the recipient's meaningful exercise of his own rights of speech, press, and political freedom" (*Board of Education v. Pico*, 1982, p. 867). In order to produce or create speech, one must have access to others' speech, which can then inform or shape one's own ideas (Balkin, 2004; Scanlon, 1972).

Our thoughts are not formed in a vacuum but are influenced and molded by all of the expressions and speech around us. For example, you may wonder about the ethics of artificial intelligence (AI) in the workplace. To form an opinion, you will probably read blogs, academic articles, and news stories; listen to the radio or podcasts; or watch videos or news shows. You would likely have conversation with others to hear different opinions and perspectives. All of this various input will help you form an opinion, which can then be shared with others. The value of your opinion is *enhanced* by having access to other information.

In fact, the scholar Thomas Emerson (1970) argued that "the right to read, listen, or see is so elemental, so close to the source of all freedom, that one can hardly conceive of a system of free expression that does not extend it full protection" (p. 6). In this perspective, receiving or accessing information and expressing information "are properly viewed as two halves of the same whole" (Cohen, 1996, p. 1006; see also Coase, 1974; Napoli, 1999; Smolla, 1992). If our freedom of speech is protected, then so are the inherent antecedents to that speech (namely, access to others' speech).

Set in this context, the court cases described previously define and demonstrate the connection between information access and freedom of speech. These two concepts go hand in hand. In addition, libraries are closely intertwined with these concepts.

LIBRARIES AND THE RIGHT TO ACCESS INFORMATION

Libraries have an important role to play regarding the right to access information: providing access to information is one of the primary purposes of most libraries. While this is codified in many statements and librarian core values (as discussed in subsequent chapters), it has been demonstrated in several court cases, in addition to *Board of Education v. Pico* (1982), which was discussed earlier.

In *Kreimer v. Bureau of Police for Morristown* (1992), a homeless person challenged a public library's rules for how patrons had to behave in the library. The rules for patron conduct included prohibitions on staring, offensive odors, being boisterous, and so on. Repeated violation of the rules could lead a patron to be banned permanently from the library.

This case did not make it to the Supreme Court but was tried in the Second District Federal Court. That court's judges said, "The First Amendment does not merely prohibit the government from enacting laws that censor information, but additionally encompasses the positive right of public access to information and ideas" (p. 1255). The court added that a public library is "the quintessential locus of the receipt of information" (p. 1256), and thus the defendant could not be barred permanently from the library. The individual's right to access information in the library outweighed the library's rules, and the homeless person won the challenge.

Similarly, Bell (2001) argued that "libraries are the archetypal traditional government-funded loci for *acquiring knowledge* just as streets and parks are by tradition archetypal government-funded loci for speaking" (p. 221, emphasis added; see also Blitz, 2006). In other words, the courts have provided strong protection for freedom of speech in public parks and streets, arguing that these spaces are key places to exercise our freedom of speech by speaking publicly. In the same way, Bell said, libraries should be seen as a key place to exercise our freedom of speech by accessing information.

This principle was tested in *Sund v. City of Wichita Falls, Texas* (2000). Two children's books, supportive of lesbian, gay, bisexual, and transgender (LGBT) families, were purchased and placed in the children's section of the public library. The books were *Heather Has Two Mommies* by Leslea Newman and *Daddy's Roommate* by Michael Willhoite. Some members of the community objected to the presence of these two books in the local public library and, through a city council resolution, forced the library director to relocate these books to the adult section.

However, other community members countered this resolution, suing to allow the library director to place the books in the appropriate section. The city council resolution was overturned because the court decided that placing these children's books in the adult section essentially cut off access to them.

In a 2002 case in Colorado (*Tattered Cover, Inc. v. City of Thornton*), a bookstore challenged a search warrant from the police, which sought information about who bought certain books. The bookstore, Tattered Cover, thought the warrant was too broad and asked for too much information. In this case, the court found that citizens have a right to receive ideas and information. The court further held:

> It is well established that [the First Amendment] safeguards a wide spectrum of activities, including . . . most importantly to this case, the right to receive information and ideas. . . . Without the right to receive information and ideas, the protection of speech under the United States and Colorado Constitutions would be meaningless. (pp. 1052–1053)

Although this case was about a bookstore, its relevance to libraries is clear: the First Amendment unequivocally includes the right to access information and ideas, which is central to libraries' purpose.

This was followed by a 2003 case, *Neinast v. Board of Trustees of the Columbus Metropolitan Library*, in which an individual who frequently went barefoot was expelled from his local public library. He successfully challenged this rule and got it overturned. The court in this case explicitly recognized a right to access information, which "includes the right to some level of access to a public library, the quintessential locus of the receipt of information" (p. 590). Again, the patron's right to access information was considered more important than library rules.

The case *United States v. American Library Association* (2003) also focused on access to information. At issue was the Children's Internet Protection Act (CIPA; 2000), a law that requires the use of internet filters in public schools and public libraries that receive certain federal funds (see Chapter 10 for a fuller exploration of internet filters). The goal of the law was to prevent minors from accessing inappropriate information online (specifically, information that is "harmful to minors").

However, the American Library Association (ALA) argued that internet filters (particularly in public libraries) would restrict adults' ability to access perfectly legal information. Nearly everything that could be described as potentially "harmful to minors" (other than obscenity) is protected by the First Amendment. In response, the government argued that the internet filters could be turned off if an adult requested it for "bona fide research" purposes.

Although the constitutionality of internet filtering was upheld by the Supreme Court, Klinefelter (2010) noted that "eight of the Justices found the ability of adult patrons to gain access to protected Internet speech to be important to the constitutionality of the library's use of internet filters" (p. 362). In other words, the ability of adults to access information (by requesting the internet filter be turned off) was an important consideration in finding CIPA constitutional. Thus, the Supreme Court recognized that access to information was an important right that needed to be considered and balanced with the impulse to protect children.

OVERARCHING THEMES

Throughout these cases, there are several important themes. One is that the reasons for wanting information (such as education, curiosity, boredom, benign or malicious intent) do not matter, legally. Individuals have the right to access information as a core part of the freedom of speech, and librarians (or other individuals) do not have the right to ask *why* people are seeking the information they want.

The second important theme is that the First Amendment right to access information needs to be balanced with other valuable considerations, such as a safe library environment or protecting minors from harmful information. However, because accessing information is a constitutional right, it is a very strong right. Often, these other considerations are not as strong as the First Amendment. For example, libraries may make rules about appropriate patron conduct, but often these rules won't hold up under First Amendment scrutiny (e.g., in the cases of *Kreimer v. Bureau of Police for Morristown* [1992] and *Neinast v. Board of Trustees of the Columbus Metropolitan Library* [2003]).

Third, the library-related cases described here all have dealt with individuals' rights to freely access information in *public* libraries, but the ideals are applicable in various degrees to all types of libraries (see Chapter 5 for specific examples of how the right to access information applies in different types of libraries).

CONCLUSION

As this chapter has shown, the right to freedom of speech, protected by the First Amendment, encompasses a right to receive or access information. This right to access information has been articulated in several court cases, including at the Supreme Court level. Access to information is an "inherent corollary" to freedom of speech for two reasons. First, it flows logically from a speaker's right to speak (there must be someone to speak to). Second, access can empower or help create our own speech and expression. This right to receive information is especially significant for libraries, which have been called the "quintessential locus" for accessing information.

NOTES

1. The exact parameters of "speech" are beyond the scope of this book, but when the word "speech" is used here, it should be understood that it refers to a wide range of expressions.

2 *Griswold v. Connecticut* (1965) focused on the rights of *married* couples to obtain such information. This right, of course, was soon expanded to all individuals.

REFERENCES

Balkin, J. M. (2004). Digital speech and democratic culture: A theory of freedom of expression for the information society. *New York University Law Review, 79,* 1–55.

Bell, B. W. (2001). Filth, filtering, and the First Amendment: Ruminations on public libraries' use of internet filtering software. *Federal Communications Law Journal, 53*(2), 191–237.

Blitz, M. J. (2006). Constitutional safeguards for silent experiments in living: Libraries, the right to read, and a First Amendment theory for an unaccompanied right to receive information. *University of Missouri-Kansas City Law Review, 74,* 799–882.

Board of Education, Island Trees Union Free School District No. 26 v. Pico, 457 U.S. 853 (1982).

Bollinger, L. C. (1986). *The tolerant society: Freedom of speech and extremist speech in America.* New York, NY: Oxford University Press.

Braddon Mitchell, D., & West, C. (2004). What is free speech? *The Journal of Political Philosophy, 12*(4), 437–460.

Burden, P. R. (2000). The key to intellectual freedom is universal access to information. *American Libraries,* 46–49.

Children's Internet Protection Act (2000), Pub. L. 106–554.

Coase, R. H. (1974). The market for goods and the market for ideas. *American Economic Review, 64*, 384–391.

Cohen, J. (1996). A right to read anonymously: A closer look at "copyright management" in cyberspace. *Connecticut Law Review, 28*, 981–1039.

Emerson, T. I. (1970). *The system of freedom of expression.* New York, NY: Vintage Books.

Griswold v. Connecticut, 382 U.S. 479 (1965).

Jones, B. M. (1999). *Libraries, access, and intellectual freedom: Developing policies for public and academic libraries.* Chicago, IL: American Library Association.

Klinefelter, A. (2010). First Amendment limits on library collection management. *Law Library Journal, 102*(3), 343–374.

Kreimer v. Bureau of Police for Morristown, 958 F.2d 1242 (1992).

Lamont v. Postmaster General, 381 U.S. 301 (1965).

Mart, S. N. (2003). The right to receive information. *Law Library Journal, 95*(2), 175–189.

Martin v. City of Struthers, 319 U.S. 141 (1943).

Napoli, P. M. (1999). The marketplace of ideas metaphor in communications regulation. *Journal of Communication, 49*(4), 151–169.

Neinast v. Board of Trustees of the Columbus Metropolitan Library, 541 U.S. 990 (2003).

Richmond Newspapers, Inc. v. Virginia, 448 U.S. 555 (1980).

Scanlon, T. M. (1972). A theory of freedom of expression. *Philosophy & Public Affairs, 1*, 204–226.

Smolla, R. A. (1992). *Free speech in an open society.* New York, NY: Knopf Books.

Smolla, R. A. (1993). Freedom of speech for libraries and librarians. *Law Library Journal, 85*, 71–79.

Smolla, R. A. (2005). *Smolla and Nimmer on freedom of speech* (Vols. I and II). Danvers, MA: Thomson/West.

Stanley v. Georgia, 394 U.S. 557 (1969).

Sund v. City of Wichita Falls, Texas, 121 F. Supp. 2d 530 (2000).

Tattered Cover v. City of Thornton, 44 P.3d 1044 (2002).

Thomas v. Collins, 323 U.S. 515 (1945).

United States v. American Library Association, 539 U.S. 194 (2003).

U.S. Constitution. Amend. I.

TWO

Three Theories behind Access to Information

This chapter traces some of the theoretical background to access to information. It is important to have a thorough grounding in the theoretical background because it can inform how we interpret current events and actions. For example, when the Supreme Court was debating the First Amendment implications of internet filters, the justices reviewed historical court cases and interpretations.

Unfortunately, access to information can often come under threat. This happens when the inclusion of a particular book or item in a library is challenged or when restrictive internet filtering is chosen. It happens when the federal government decides to not publish certain scientific data that contradict current government policy. It happens when libraries decide they are not going to purchase items that might make some of their patrons uncomfortable.

When these sorts of things occur, our defense of access is strengthened by understanding its theoretical roots. We can formulate better

Portions of this chapter are reprinted from Shannon M. Oltmann, "Intellectual Freedom and Freedom of Speech: Three Theoretical Perspectives," *The Library Quarterly* 86, no. 2 (April 2016): 153–171.

rebuttals to repression of information when we thoroughly grasp the importance of access. This chapter briefly explains how to understand legal theory before delineating the three main legal theories supporting information access.

THE BACKGROUND OF LEGAL THEORY

Legal theory is a type of scholarship that attempts to explain court cases and provide theoretical explanations for the rulings of the court system. Most legal (or jurisprudence) theory is based on an examination of court decisions and writings. This makes it different than scientific theories, which are based on stating hypotheses, variables, and findings. As the *Blackwell Guide to the Philosophy of Law and Legal Theory* states, legal theory "has tended to concentrate on rationalizing and legitimating whole departments of legal doctrine" (Edmundson, 2005, p. 1; see also Barzun, 2007; Blasi, 1977; Shiffrin, 2011). Rodney Smolla (2005) suggested,

> "Free speech theory" refers to various attempts by jurists and schol-ars to supply answers to what might be called the *Why* question implicit in the First Amendment. Why does the First Amendment exist? What is the purpose of freedom of speech? (pp. 2–3, emphasis in original)

In other words, legal theories include different ways to understand, inter-pret, and apply the concept of "freedom of speech." In this chapter, we have a similar focus. We are focused on the freedom of speech—specifically, how and why the freedom of speech includes access to information.

There are several theories that support and explain how U.S. courts have conceptualized freedom of speech, but three of them are used most frequently: the marketplace of ideas, democracy, and individual utility. (See Table 2.1 for a brief summary of each theory.)

Several scholars note that utilizing multiple theories for freedom of speech is reasonable and powerful. Even the Supreme Court itself does not have a single overarching theory (Hopkins, 1996; Schauer, 1982; Shiffrin, 2011); it draws on multiple theories, depending on which one is most rele-vant and useful. Thus, this chapter argues that the three theories discussed here—the marketplace of ideas, democracy, and individual utility—are all valuable, important, and useful ways to theorize freedom of speech and access to information.

Table 2.1 Summary of Three Predominant Legal Theories about Freedom of Speech

Theoretical Approach	Key Arguments
The marketplace of ideas	• Ideas should compete with one another in a marketplace, in which the best (most truthful) ideas will eventually be adopted. • Speakers are analogous to sellers and listeners to buyers/consumers. • Full or partial truth can be found in most ideas, so all should be heard. • Even falsehoods can aid the search for truth by strengthening true arguments. • Ideas are evaluated through ongoing, community-engaging processes.
Democracy	• Free speech is essential to promoting and ensuring democracy. • Free speech is implicated in both civic participation and public deliberation. • It ensures that citizens know their rights and can exercise them. • Free speech keeps government accountable and responsive. • It facilitates good collective decision-making.
Individual utility/ autonomy	• Freedom of speech (thought) is essential to self-fulfillment and development. • It can empower individuals. • Free speech is an end in itself.

MARKETPLACE OF IDEAS

The "marketplace of ideas" is one of the predominant theories concerning the right to freedom of speech (Braddon-Mitchell & West, 2004; Gordon, 1997; Hopkins, 1996; Napoli, 1999; Smolla, 2005). Usually, the marketplace of ideas is combined with the "search for truth" approach, and they are treated as one unified theory. They are stronger and more fruitful together.

The Search for Truth

The search for truth[1] simply means that people (at least theoretically) seek to figure out the facts or truth about a wide range of topics. For example, if someone wanted to know whether climate change is responsible for more frequent and intense hurricanes, that person would, presumably, try to find the truth about the matter. He or she, for instance, might read reports from the Intergovernmental Panel on Climate Change—an international group of scientists who study climate change. This person might search for academic articles about hurricane intensity, read and watch news reports, and seek out experts, all in an attempt to find the truth.

This legal theory assumes that people are going to seek the *truth* rather than trying to find, say, information that only confirms their beliefs or only searching for the easiest-to-find information. Unfortunately, we know from research that people do often seek easy-to-find information and often look for information that confirms their beliefs rather than looking for the objective truth.

For the sake of this argument, though, we can imagine that people are concerned primarily with seeking truth. And, when looked at holistically, we can see that the overall arc of humanity bends toward discovering and verifying truth (consider our changing views about whether Earth is the center of the universe).

In the classic book *On Liberty* (1869), John Stuart Mill argued that allowing free speech is the best way to ensure the advancement of truth. The basic idea is that, if we have free speech, many ideas will be suggested and debated, and over time, the best ideas will gain support and rise to the top. In this scenario, the marketplace of ideas is a (figurative) place in which truth emerges from an engaging, interactive competition. The open and free exchange of ideas will lead to the eventual adoption of the best ideas, which win out over falsehoods.

Holmes's Famous Dissent

Mill's (1869) ideas were echoed in Justice Oliver Wendell Holmes's famous dissent in *Abrams v. United States* (1919). In this case, two activists were convicted of circulating antiwar pamphlets in violation of the law at that time. The Supreme Court upheld the conviction, but Holmes disagreed with that.

Instead, he argued that the government did not have the right to silence opposition; his view was later adopted by the Supreme Court (which, after this case, has generally given stronger leeway to antiwar activists). In fact, Holmes's dissent in *Abrams v. United States* (1919) is the foundation of modern legal understandings of freedom of speech. Holmes argued that the best test of truth is

> the power of the thought to get itself accepted in the competition of the market, and that truth is the only ground upon which [citizens'] wishes safely can be carried out. That at any rate is the theory of our Constitution. (p. 630)

In this metaphor, "speakers are analogous to producers and sellers, [and] listeners and viewers are analogous to buyers and consumers" (Riley, 2005, p. 164). Speakers offer opinions, ideas, and information; listeners evaluate the multiple ideas available and choose what they think will be most meaningful or useful.

According to Mill and Holmes, people should choose the best, the most truthful, information (even though we know this is not necessarily how people actually act). While each individual person may not choose the most truthful and best information, these authors believed that humanity, over time, would generally choose the truth.

Foundational freedom of speech cases, such as *Lamont v. Postmaster General* (1965) and *Griswold v. Connecticut* (1965; discussed in Chapter 1), utilized the marketplace of ideas to explain why individuals' freedom of speech needs to be protected. In *Lamont v. Postmaster General*, people challenged a law about information related to communism. At the time, there was great fear about the spread of communism, so there was a federal law that the post office could hold any communist mailing and only had to deliver it if people specifically agreed to receive it. The idea was to reduce the circulation of communist information.

In this case, Justice William Brennan articulated the relationship between freedom of speech and access to information, writing,

> it is true that the First Amendment contains no specific guarantee of access to publications. However, the protection of the Bill of Rights goes beyond the specific guarantees to protect from congressional abridgment those equally fundamental personal rights necessary to

> make the express guarantees fully meaningful. . . . The dissemina-
> tion of ideas can accomplish nothing if otherwise willing addressees
> are not free to receive and consider them. It would be a barren mar-
> ketplace of ideas that had only sellers and no buyers. (p. 308)

Brennan thus explained that freedom of speech has little power if others cannot receive, or access, that speech. A marketplace without buyers, he speculates, would soon become a marketplace without sellers, thus elimi-nating the purpose of and need for a market. The ability to "buy"—to access information—is necessary to constitute a market.

Understanding the Market as a Metaphor

As Napoli (1999) noted, "By the mid-1960s, the marketplace metaphor had fully crystallized into a concise expression of a key dimension of the First Amendment" (p. 155). Vincent Blasi (1997), a noted First Amend-ment scholar, argued that the marketplace of ideas should be understood *symbolically*; he made this argument because he saw this metaphor as the best explanation for freedom of speech jurisprudence.

Blasi noted that the social values of ideas and information are not cap-tured in *economic* descriptions of markets; instead, Blasi demonstrated that Holmes had a more nuanced market in mind. He wrote, "Ideas should be evaluated the way consumer goods and services are: not by any kind of political or intellectual authority but rather by an open-ended process that measures and integrates the ongoing valuations of all the individuals" (1997, p. 4).

Thus, individuals, through their consideration, rejection, and selection of ideas, demonstrate which ideas have the most currency, power, and importance (or, in Mill's conception, truth). In this manner, ideas are sub-jected to "a vibrant, brutal weeding-out process analogous to the func-tions markets for goods and services perform" (Blasi, 2004, p. 24). In fact, this weeding-out process is a widely recognized approach; Volokh (2011) noted that "the constant process of questioning, testing, updating, and sometimes replacing received wisdom is the hallmark of good science and good history" (p. 597).

Consider the pseudoscience of phrenology. Several scientists from the 1700s through the 1900s argued that you could figure out a person's char-acteristics and personality from the shapes of bumps on his or her head (for a brief overview, go to the Encyclopedia Britannica (2018) entry: https://

www.britannica.com/topic/phrenology). This idea has been subjected to rigorous debate and study over centuries and, as a result, has been thoroughly debunked. This demonstrates the power of the marketplace of ideas to evaluate ideas and reject those that are lacking.

As Blasi (2004) cautioned, the market should be understood as a metaphor. Thus, Gordon's (1997) concern that truth does not survive under economic market conditions misses the point: Holmes was not suggesting we submit ideas to an economic market but rather to similar processes, uncontrolled by authority and open to collective evaluation (see also Smolla, 2005).

Hopkins (1996) provided some empirical evidence that this perspective of free speech has been taken up by the Supreme Court. After surveying how the Supreme Court employed the phrase "marketplace of ideas," Hopkins noted that "members of the Court have referred to a multitude of marketplaces and have indicated that these marketplaces are controlled by differing technology, geography, content, or other factors" (p. 45). In other words, there are *multiple* marketplaces, which are overlapping, disorganized, and unpredictable.

The marketplace of ideas metaphor has endured since being introduced into American jurisprudence by Holmes. It has been used in at least 125 opinions in ninety-seven cases involving free speech issues between 1919 and 1995 (Hopkins, 1996). In addition, the marketplace of ideas has gained acceptance beyond legal theorists, becoming known in popular culture.

DEMOCRACY AND FREE SPEECH

The marketplace of ideas theory is often tied to the argument from democracy—the second predominant theory concerning freedom of speech. According to this line of thinking, freedom of speech is crucial because it enables the circulation of ideas and accountability necessary to a healthy democracy.

Emerson (1970) explained that "the governed must, in order to exercise their right of consent, have full freedom of expression both in forming individual judgments and in forming the common judgment" (p. 7). In other words, the people in a democracy need freedom of speech to develop and express their ideas among each other and to their representatives in the government. Citizens of a democracy need as much information as possible to make good political decisions.

Political Speech

Most formulations of the democracy theory of free speech are concerned primarily or exclusively with political speech, which is any "citizen's speech, press, peaceable assembly, or petition, whenever those activities are utilized for the governing of the nation" (Meiklejohn, 1961, p. 256). The speech that is most directly connected to democracy is the most strongly protected, under this theory. For example, this would strongly protect protests that were political in nature, letters to one's congressperson or the president, political speeches in a park, and so on.

Critics have charged that this theory applies *only* to political speech, overlooking or discounting many other types of speech and forms of expression, particularly popular culture (Balkin, 2004; Schauer, 1982, 1986). Would the democracy theory protect, for example, a rap song? Poetry? Children's books? There is a lot of speech that is not political in nature but is still important to people in one way or another.

However, Meiklejohn (1961), the father of this theory, extended political speech to include education, philosophy and science, general public discussions, and literature and the arts. He felt all of these areas were important contributors to forming robust and meaningful political speech. The Supreme Court has rejected the idea that First Amendment protection is only for political speech (while also recognizing the importance of political speech) (Smolla, 2005).

Nevertheless, it is not clear how far we can stretch "political speech" without weakening the emphasis on democracy (Schauer, 1986; Smolla, 2005). This is a potential weakness of this theory.

Importance of Public Deliberation and Participation

Regardless of the specific types of speech that may be covered by this theory, "public deliberation [is seen] as a cornerstone of participatory democracy and representative government" (Delli Carpini, Cook, & Jacobs, 2004, p. 316). In other words, discussing political ideas and perspectives with one another is perhaps the most important part of our form of government. It is one of the best ways to ensure that we consider different points of view.

Smolla (1992) explained that there are five ways that self-governance (in other words, democracy) and free speech are connected. First, freedom of speech is "a means of participation, the vehicle through which individuals debate the issues of the day, cast their votes, and actively join in the processes of decision-making" inherent in a democracy (p. 12). Free speech itself enables participation in democracy.

Second, in an argument derivative of the marketplace of ideas, freedom of speech aids in the pursuit of political truth (Smolla, 1992). For example, you might hear arguments about "trickle down" economics, "trickle up" economics, socialism, and other forms of economic management. Listening to or reading about these various ideas, as well as discussing them with others, can help you move closer to "political truth."

The Freedom to Read Statement from the American Library Association (ALA) also connects the marketplace of ideas and the democracy theories: "Most attempts at suppression [or censorship] rest on a denial of the fundamental premise of democracy: that the ordinary individual, by exercising critical judgment, will select the good and reject the bad" (ALA, 2006, para. 2). In other words, this statement is saying that our democracy rests on the marketplace of ideas.

Third, free speech can aid majority rule by "ensuring that collective policy-making represents, to the greatest degree possible, the collective will" (Smolla, 1992, p. 12). How would politicians be able to implement what people want, if people were unable (or unwilling) to voice their preferences? The people have to be able to articulate what they want their representatives to enact in law.

Smolla's (1992) fourth point was that free speech can be a restraint on state tyranny and corruption. If a political leader was being tyrannical, people could be outspoken against that, through political protest, for example. Protest might lead to a turnover in political leadership or in the leader behaving more appropriately. Sometimes the knowledge that people *could* protest is enough, in a democracy, to limit tyrannical actions.

Finally, according to Smolla (1992), free speech provides stability in a democracy by ensuring that minority views are heard. Because everyone has freedom of speech, even those in the minority or with unpopular views can express their perspectives. If not, they might become so frustrated and disenfranchised that they rebelled against the government.

Problems with Public Participation

However, the low levels of political participation and the modern complexity of most democracies counter simplistic, deterministic relationships between information and democracy. In other words, more information does not automatically equal a better democracy. In fact, more information can confuse and mislead people, creating complications for a democracy.

And allowing more freedom of speech does not mean that people will use it at *all*, let alone use it *responsibly* to improve their democracy. After reviewing all of the recent research on deliberative democracy, Delli Carpini et al. (2004) concluded that

> countering the optimism of proponents of deliberative democracy is a strong and persistent suspicion that public deliberation is so infrequent, unrepresentative, subject to conscious manipulation and unconscious bias, and disconnected from actual decision making as to make it at best an impractical mechanism for determining the public will, and at worst misleading or dangerous. (p. 321)

These researchers found that public deliberation of political ideas generally did not live up to the ideals. People were likely to fall for either manipulation or bias, according to research.

This bleak outlook was written even before the power of the internet and social media really influenced political campaigns and decision-making. With political knowledge among individuals steadily decreasing, some scholars suggest that the democratic ideal of engaged citizens is no longer realistic.

It is difficult to evaluate the significance of the democracy theory of freedom of speech. On one hand, it remains theoretically and normatively significant. It continues to shape how we view our democracy and how we think our democracy ought to work. We think freedom of speech should be an important component of a well-functioning democracy. On the other hand, we see evidence that freedom of speech doesn't really work like that.

INDIVIDUAL UTILITY/AUTONOMY

The third predominant legal theory about freedom of speech argues that freedom of speech is important because it helps create and empower individual self-fulfillment. One of the big proponents of this approach wrote,

> Freedom of expression is essential as a means of assuring individual self-fulfillment. The proper end of man [*sic*] is the realization of his [*sic*] character and potentialities as a human being. For the

achievement of this self-realization the mind must be free. Hence suppression of belief, opinion, or other expression is . . . a negation of man's [*sic*] essential nature. (Emerson, 1970, p. 6)

In other words, we need freedom of speech to come to our full potential as humans. This theory posits that freedom of speech "is a right defiantly, robustly, and irreverently to speak one's mind *just because it is one's mind*" (Smolla, 1993, p. 9, emphasis in original).[2]

In the 1969 case *Red Lion Broadcasting v. FCC*, the Supreme Court referred to the theory of individual autonomy. In this case, the Red Lion Broadcasting Company challenged the Federal Communications Commission's (FCC) fairness doctrine, but the justices upheld the doctrine. Justice Byron White wrote that "the right of the public to receive suitable access to social, political, esthetic, moral, and other ideas and experiences is crucial" (p. 390). Here, the court argued that citizens need access to diverse ideas for personal fulfillment and enlightenment.

Varied Interpretations of the Individual Autonomy Argument

Brison (1998) articulated several distinct but related variations of the autonomy argument, some of which are described here. First, autonomy can be seen from the perspective of Mill (1869), as "freedom of governmental interference in some specified domain" (Brison, 1998, p. 324). In this sense, autonomy simply means that we are not interfered with but are free to do as we please (within the bounds of the law). Freedom of speech enhances our ability to do so.

A second version of autonomy argues that "autonomous persons could not allow the state to protect them against the harm of coming to have false beliefs" without losing their autonomy (Brison, 1998, p. 327; see also Scanlon, 1972). If we are truly free, that means we are free to adopt whatever beliefs we want, even false beliefs.

Some people believe that the moon landings were a hoax perpetuated by the U.S. government; though this is demonstrably false, they are free to believe whatever they like. If the government tried to prevent us from adopting and arguing for false information, then it would be infringing on our freedom. (This argument can get complicated when someone's false beliefs start impacting the health or welfare of others.)

A third perspective on autonomy perceives it as an "ability to be rationally self-legislating" (Brison, 1998, p. 330). This means that we have the ability (and the right) to regulate ourselves, in terms of what we think and articulate.

Finally, another perspective comes from Robertson (2011), who explained that the First Amendment "protects those of us who may have no inclination to make our views known to the world, but would rather silently sample the many viewpoints that others make available to us" (p. 324).

This view aligns well with libraries. Here, Robertson (2011) argued that freedom of speech is not always for speaking your mind out loud. It is also for considering other points of view, silently, in your own mind. He went on to say,

> This right allows both those without the confidence to make their views publicly known and those with no viewpoint at all to develop a unique viewpoint. This chance for intellectual exploration and individual self-examination free from fear of government interference is exactly what the First Amendment is [for]. (p. 328)

The right to access information in a library can allow people to think, imagine, create, and fully realize themselves.

CONCLUSION

In this chapter, we have discussed three different legal theories that explain and justify freedom of speech in the United States. All three of these theories are useful in slightly different contexts.

For example, if your library is trying to explain why it contains many different perspectives on a topic, using the marketplace of ideas metaphor would probably be the most appropriate. Holding programming events relating to voting rights, for example, could be justified with the theory of democracy. Finally, a library might use the theory of individual autonomy to defend parts of its nonfiction section, which help individuals think through and decide on important issues. Together, these three theories provide a robust defense of the freedom of speech.

It is important to be familiar with these legal theories. They provide the foundation and justification for our freedom of speech, which is connected to the basic purpose of libraries, providing access to information. As discussed in Chapter 1, access to information is part of freedom of speech. Thus, knowing these legal theories gives you a good understanding of why access to information is so important.

NOTES

1. This argument sidesteps the question of whether there is a single, objective "truth" out there. Many social scientists, for example, would question this assumption. For the sake of understanding this argument, however, we do not need to settle this question.

2. The argument from autonomy may be particularly a Western view. The West (Europe and North America) tends to place more emphasis on individualism and self-fulfillment than the East does, philosophically.

REFERENCES

Abrams v. United States, 250 U.S. 616 (1919).

American Library Association. (2006). Freedom to read statement. Retrieved from http://www.ala.org/advocacy/intfreedom/freedomreadstatement. Document ID: aaac95d4-2988-0024-6573-10a5ce6b21b2.

Balkin, J. M. (2004). Digital speech and democratic culture: A theory of freedom of expression for the information society. *New York University Law Review, 79*, 1–55.

Barzun, C. L. (2007). Politics or principle? Zechariah Chafee and the social interest in free speech. *Brigham Young University Law Review, 2007*(2), 259–325.

Blasi, V. (1977). The checking value in First Amendment theory. *American Bar Foundation Research Journal, 2*(3), 521–649.

Blasi, V. (1997). *Propter honoris respectum*: Reading Holmes through the lens of Schauer: The Abrams dissent. *Notre Dame Law Review, 72*, 1343–1361.

Blasi, V. (2004). Holmes and the marketplace of ideas. *Supreme Court Review, 2004*, 1–46.

Braddon-Mitchell, D., & West, C. (2004). What is free speech? *The Journal of Political Philosophy, 12*(4), 437–460.

Brison, S. J. (1998). The autonomy defense of free speech. *Ethics, 108*(2), 312–339.

Delli Carpini, M. X., Cook, F. L., & Jacobs, L. R. (2004). Public deliberation, discursive participation, and citizen engagement: A review of the empirical literature. *Annual Review of Political Science, 7*, 315–344.

Edmundson, W. A. (2005). *The Blackwell guide to the philosophy of law and legal theory*. Malden, MA: Blackwell Publishing.

Emerson, T. I. (1970). *The system of freedom of expression.* New York, NY: Vintage Books.

Encyclopedia Britannica. (2018). Phrenology. Retrieved from https://www.britannica.com/topic/phrenology

Gordon, J. (1997). John Stuart Mill and the "marketplace of ideas." *Social Theory & Practice, 23*(2), 235–249.

Griswold v. Connecticut, 382 U.S. 479 (1965).

Hopkins, W. W. (1996). The Supreme Court defines the marketplace of ideas. *Journalism & Mass Communication Quarterly, 73*(1), 40–52.

Lamont v. Postmaster General, 381 U.S. 301 (1965).

Meiklejohn, A. (1961). The First Amendment is an absolute. *Supreme Court Review, 1961*, 245–266.

Mill, J. S. (1869/1921). *On liberty.* London, England: Longmans, Green, & Co.

Napoli, P. M. (1999). The marketplace of ideas metaphor in communications regulation. *Journal of Communication, 49*(4), 151–169.

Oltmann, S. M. (2016). Intellectual freedom and freedom of speech: Three theoretical perspectives. *Library Quarterly, 86*(2), 153–171.

Red Lion Broadcasting Co. v. FCC, 395 U.S. 367 (1969).

Riley, J. (2005). J.S. Mill's doctrine of freedom of expression. *Utilitas, 17*(2), 147–179.

Robertson, E. (2011). A fundamental right to read: Reader privacy protections in the U.S. Constitution. *University of Colorado Law Review, 82*, 307–330.

Scanlon, T. M. (1972). A theory of freedom of expression. *Philosophy & Public Affairs, 1*, 204–226.

Schauer, F. (1982). *Free speech: A philosophical enquiry.* Cambridge, England: Cambridge University Press.

Schauer, F. (1986). The role of the people in First Amendment theory. *California Law Review, 74*, 761–788.

Shiffrin, S. (2011). Dissent, democratic participation, and First Amendment methodology. *Virginia Law Review, 67*, 559–565.

Smolla, R. A. (1992). *Free speech in an open society.* New York, NY: Knopf Books.

Smolla, R. A. (1993). Freedom of speech for libraries and librarians. *Law Library Journal, 85*, 71–79.

Smolla, R. A. (2005). *Smolla and Nimmer on freedom of speech* (Vols. I and II). Danvers, MA: Thomson/West.

Volokh, E. (2011). In defense of the marketplace of ideas/search for truth as a theory of free speech protection. *Virginia Law Review, 97*(3), 595–601.

THREE

The Freedom to Explore

In the first two chapters, we explored the importance of freedom of speech and its connection to one of the main goals of most libraries, providing access to information. In this chapter, we look at access to information from a slightly different perspective: the freedom to explore. Although the freedom to explore is not explicitly enshrined in the U.S. Constitution, it is nonetheless an important part of our contemporary society.

This chapter explains one of the reasons that intellectual freedom is essential: everyone needs freedom to explore new ideas, concepts, and perspectives. We explore the theoretical and practical importance of this idea and demonstrate its function in our contemporary society.

WHAT DO WE MEAN BY "FREEDOM TO EXPLORE"?

Blitz (2006) called the freedom to explore the "right to silently quarry or sample public culture for information that will enlighten, enrich, or simply entertain" (p. 800). From this initial definition, we can see that the freedom to explore is not solely about intellectual pursuits—that is, we do not need to be searching for educational or informative resources to be utilizing this freedom. We can be exploring ideas for pleasure and recreation as well.

The Supreme Court has implied this as well. In *Stanley v. Georgia* (1969), the Supreme Court noted that the "right to receive information and ideas, regardless of their social worth . . . is fundamental to our free society" (p. 564). *Any* sort of search, including those for pleasure or recreation, can be supported by the argument for freedom to explore. Searches for information that might be repugnant can be included too. As a result, the freedom to explore should be understood very broadly.

For example, someone may want to hear different varieties of jazz music, just to sample the diversity of sounds. Having the freedom to explore means that person does not need to justify or defend his or her search but can freely examine whatever seems interesting. Perhaps exploring the world of jazz leads the person to bebop or soul music. Perhaps the person becomes attached to one particular performer and follows the twists and turns of his or her career. Or perhaps he or she becomes bored with jazz and turns to early rock instead. All of these (and an endless number of other options) are supported by the freedom to explore.

Of course, the freedom to explore *does* often encompass intellectual or information-gathering pursuits as well. Someone may want to know about energy production and consumption in the United States, for example. There are many resources with diverse perspectives and arguments on such a topic. People in the library should feel free to explore these many different options.

At the same time, people do not have an obligation or expectation to explore *all* the options or only the *best* options. That sort of framework would be inherently restrictive, limiting people to someone's idea of the "best" information. That would be counter to the ideals of intellectual freedom and freedom of speech, which push for more access to more information.

This does mean that sometimes people will find (or settle for) less-than-ideal sources. Perhaps the person searching for information about energy production reads only about solar power and does not find information about hydroelectric, coal, natural gas, or other sources of energy.

While such a limited perspective may not be ideal, it is perfectly acceptable within the framework of freedom to explore and the framework of intellectual freedom. Again, the purpose of the freedom to explore is, simply, freedom—and sometimes people will use their freedom in ways we might not agree with.

A LACK OF JUDGMENT

The freedom to explore also encompasses ideas and perspectives that may be unpopular, controversial, awkward, embarrassing, or even unwelcome in public discussion and debate. It is not just for ideas that are safe, bland, and well-accepted.

Let's imagine a patron was interested in learning more about cults. There may be many reasons for such an interest, some benign and some less so. The freedom to explore, though, applies regardless of why someone has an interest. Whether this person was in a cult, has a loved one in a cult, wants to avoid cults, wants to start a cult, studies government responses to cults, or has yet another reason for the interest is actually immaterial when exploring a topic—especially while in a library.

Within the freedom to explore is a lack of judgment. Any and all reasons to investigate a topic are acceptable, just as any and all topics are. We have to suspend possible personal and professional opinions about both the topics a person seeks out and the reasons for seeking those topics.

One basis for this is that we cannot deduce much from what a person may choose to read or explore. Robertson (2011) explains, "People read books for an infinite variety of reasons, and drawing generalized conclusions from another's reading choices wrongly assumes that the most obvious one is always the correct one" (p. 308).

Furthermore, we do not know whether a book borrower read that book, agreed with it, and accepted the ideas in it (Kennedy, 1989). This holds true for most instances of information seeking and access—we simply do not know which portion (if any) of a magazine, CD, video, or website that a person read *or* whether the person agreed with it. We could try to draw inferences based on the content, but those inferences are likely to be superficial and incorrect.

Imagine someone does research on knitting, checking out many books and other resources. Do we now know that person is a knitter? Not really. Perhaps a family member is learning knitting, so the patron checked out books on his or her behalf. Perhaps the patron simply wants to better understand the popularity of knitting. Perhaps the patron is a crime novel writer and needs to know about the circumference of various needles to determine the perfect murder weapon for his or her next book.

There are so many inferences we could draw, and the simplest one is not necessarily most likely to be correct. It is far better to not draw inferences about patrons based on what they read, watch, or peruse. We should let them have privacy to explore whatever they want to explore.

THE FREEDOM TO EXPLORE AND LIBRARIES

Blitz (2006) focused his article on libraries as the most basic, central location for utilizing the freedom to explore. Libraries of all varieties are essential for the freedom to explore for three reasons.

First, libraries typically have large collections that are accessible to individuals (except for some special libraries and archives, which may have closed stacks). Open stacks and online catalogs facilitate browsing and exploring, freeing patrons to explore on their own without mediation from librarians. Most librarians have encountered patrons wandering the stacks, skimming titles and authors. Or patrons may explore various topics with the online catalog, which can facilitate finding related materials that may not be colocated.

In fact, many aspects of library service can be seen as aiding the freedom to explore, such as posting read-alike lists, providing readers' advisory, turning some books out on the shelves, creating displays, and so on. These services are done to help readers make connections between items and to spark their curiosity, without necessarily interacting with library staff. Patrons can explore the library's stacks freely.

Another reason that libraries are the central location for the freedom to explore is that there are few barriers to using most libraries. Usually, there are no fees to use a library and its collections, and generally anyone in the patron base is welcome to enter the building and use the collection. (While many academic and school libraries limit their patrons to current students and faculty, this is a reasonable boundary, and within this framework, they typically provide open access to their patrons.)

For patrons who cannot or do not wish to physically visit the library, they can often access some collections online, such as e-books, databases, streaming music, and so on. People without physical access or reliable internet access to the library may still be served by bookmobiles. In addition to these myriad points of access, librarians and other staff are available to answer questions and provide guidance as desired.

Finally, libraries are important to the freedom to explore because of their ethical norms and values (see Chapter 4 for an in-depth discussion of library core values). These provide a very strong grounding and defense of the freedom to explore. From the American Library Association's (ALA) statements, we can see that curiosity, learning, and recreation are important to the profession.

Central to Librarianship

Freedom to explore, though not always described in that exact phrase, is central to librarianship. The definition of intellectual freedom includes "all expressions of ideas through which any and all sides of a question, cause or movement may be explored" (ALA, 2007a, para. 1). The word "explore" is thus central to intellectual freedom. Both the Freedom to Read Statement and the Library Bill of Rights explain and defend the importance of offering many perspectives, even those that may be unpopular.

The Freedom to Read Statement (ALA, 2006b) suggests that conformity of thought is dangerous, especially in times of social tension. Instead,

> Freedom keeps open the path of novel and creative solutions, and enables change to come by choice. Every silencing of a heresy, every enforcement of an orthodoxy, diminishes the toughness and resilience of our society and leaves it the less able to deal with controversy and difference. (para. 4)

This argument implies that we need both a wide variety of ideas and the freedom to explore them without suspicion or judgment. Our society is strengthened when all ideas are able to be considered and explored. In contrast, when only certain views are allowed to be disseminated (which would be called orthodoxy), the adaptability of our society is weakened.

Likewise, the Library Bill of Rights (ALA, 2006c) emphasizes the importance of fighting against censorship and allowing a wide diversity of perspectives, noting that materials should be provided for "the interest, information, and enlightenment of all people of the community the library serves" (para. 1). That covers a wide range of reasons to have information and to pursue information—in other words, freedom to explore the diverse perspectives offered by the library.

In addition, the ALA has issued several interpretations of the Library Bill of Rights, which address the freedom to explore. For example, in "Advocating for Intellectual Freedom," the ALA states, "Libraries empower individuals to explore ideas, access and evaluate information, draw meaning from information presented in a variety of formats, develop valid conclusions, and express new ideas" (2009, para. 6).

The statement "Diversity in Collection Development" (ALA, 2006a) notes that libraries should include "materials that reflect political, economic, religious, social, minority, and sexual issues" (para. 4). Having such a wide variety of materials allows patrons to truly utilize their freedom to explore diverse ideas and perspectives. To facilitate the freedom to explore, the ALA states in "Politics in American Libraries" that

> libraries should collect, maintain, and provide access to as wide a selection of materials, reflecting as wide a diversity of views on

political topics as possible, within their budgetary constraints and local community needs. A balanced collection need not and cannot contain an equal number of resources representing every possible viewpoint on every issue. A balanced collection should include the variety of views that surround any given issue. (ALA, 2017, para. 3)

This emphasizes the importance of having many perspectives and applies not only to politics but also to all topics that may be found in the library. By having diverse and balanced collections, libraries create opportunities for patrons to exercise their freedom to explore and, as Blitz (2006) explains, offer a private enclave that allows "one to engage in *solitary* First Amendment activity rather than social discourse" (p. 827, emphasis added).

THE IMPORTANCE OF THE FREEDOM TO EXPLORE

The freedom to explore "is of fundamental importance to free thought and free expression because it provides individuals with the opportunity to engage with controversial ideas, develop intellectually, and formulate speech they intend to share with others" (Ard, 2013, p. 6). In other words, we can think about controversial ideas and develop our own unique beliefs and perspectives, because of the freedom to explore.

In fact, the Supreme Court has ruled in a few cases that one's reading material and related associations are protected speech. For example, in *United States v. Rumely* (1953), the court held that Rumely did not have to reveal who purchased materials that he published. Congress wanted to know who purchased (in bulk) the political books Rumely published, but he refused to divulge the information; his position was upheld by the Supreme Court. Although this was not about reading materials obtained from a library, the implication is that one's reading material should be legally protected.

The scholar Marc Blitz (2006) argued that the freedom to explore is especially important for people who want to conduct "thought experiments" or think through different ways of living without actually changing their lives: the freedom to explore is "invaluable in freeing numerous individuals who, for any number of reasons, cannot try out new ways of life or immerse themselves in unfamiliar ideas within the context of their community or professional role" (p. 810).

Many people daydream about living in a remote cabin in the woods, away from modern technologies and stresses. Exploring this idea online and in the library allows people to think through all the ramifications without actually quitting their job, selling their house, and becoming a hermit. The right to access multiple points of view—to explore different perspectives—is "a way for people to quietly participate in the kind of vigorous self-examination and free intellectual exploration that the First Amendment is supposed to provide" (Blitz, 2006, p. 803).

Blitz noted that this freedom is *particularly* important for those who may not want to exercise speech (i.e., words spoken out loud) and for those who cannot exercise their freedom of speech. Imagine a person who works for a nonprofit group that counsels against abortion. Due to the person's job, she is unlikely to be able to speak freely about the possible reasons one may seek an abortion and may feel uncomfortable attending a pro-choice rally. But in her spare time, she could read and think freely about different perspectives. This freedom to explore various ideas can lead, over time, to change.

Sometimes the freedom to explore ideas simply leads to more thought and contemplation, or as Blitz (2006) says, "*unmonitored* intellectual exploration" (p. 809, emphasis in original). That, in itself, is an ideal worth pursuing and protecting.

THE FREEDOM TO EXPLORE CONNECTS WITH LEGAL THEORIES

In addition, as mentioned previously, the freedom to explore helps strengthen the three theoretical foundations of the freedom of speech (described in Chapter 2). Those legal theories, again, were the marketplace of ideas, democracy, and individual autonomy.

For example, exploring new points of view can improve one's autonomy and self-worth. Someone who has considered multiple perspectives on an issue, and then decided for himself or herself, is generally more confident in his or her stance. The topic of "conspiracy theories" is perfect to illustrate this point, whether the alleged conspiracy is the murder of John F. Kennedy, the 9/11 terrorist attack, the actions of pharmaceutical companies, chemtrails, the existence of "lizard people," or some other theory.

People can read a variety of perspectives and thoughtfully consider the evidence and analysis on all sides, before determining their own point of view. Having considered all available perspectives and evidence will likely strengthen an individual's belief in his or her stance. (We can acknowledge that those who believe in conspiracy theories do not always act in such a rational manner; nonetheless, the freedom to explore allows for, and fosters, such a process.)

Being told what to believe and what to do, with no alternatives, is what happens in dystopian novels and totalitarian societies, directly undermining individual autonomy and self-fulfillment (and democracy). These values are incredibly important in our modern society and should be encouraged. The freedom to explore is central to these values.

The freedom to explore is central not only to individual autonomy but also to our contemporary conceptualization of democracy. We will learn in Chapter 4 that the right of access to information informs good democracy; people need access to a wide range of information to make good political decisions (e.g., which candidates to support, which policies to endorse). We need access not only to the ideas that others voice but also to ideas that silently circulate—and even to ideas that may not be in circulation but are sitting on a dusty shelf, waiting to be discovered.

Consider the increasingly voluminous voices calling for decriminalization of marijuana. These arguments were first encountered in quiet reading, reflection, and consideration of related facts and perspectives and then were gradually shared and gained momentum. At earlier points in U.S. history, simply suggesting out loud that marijuana be decriminalized would be met with suspicion and hostility, perhaps even a law enforcement investigation; because people contemplated such ideas gradually, a societal shift has gradually occurred. This example demonstrates that freedom to explore may lead to conversation and discussion, then public debate and analysis, and perhaps to a seismic shift in attitudes and laws.

The freedom to explore, similarly, informs the search for truth in the marketplace of ideas. Blitz (2006) says that, with the freedom to explore, "individuals are thus freer to explore idiosyncratic paths of intellectual development instead of choosing from among the more limited options likely to be prominent in collective discourse" (p. 805).

In other words, we are not restricted to only the ideas that are currently popular, but we can access a wider range of ideas and perspectives (especially in libraries). This expands the marketplace of ideas for everyone who exercises the freedom to explore.

THE IMPORTANCE OF PRIVACY FOR THE FREEDOM TO EXPLORE

Several scholars argue that the freedom to explore rests upon strong privacy protection. Richards (2008), for example, argues, "Surveillance or interference can warp the integrity of our freedom of thought and can skew the way we think, with clear repercussions for the content of our subsequent speech or writing" (p. 389).

Research has shown that if people know they are being watched, they will behave differently (Foucault, 1991). One public library in an urban area used to keep items that patrons had requested (often called "hold items") on an open shelf, marked with the patron's name. This allowed the patron to pick up the hold items he or she requested and then check them out. It *also* allowed a nosy person to snoop through the hold items and see who requested which items. In this close-knit community, a gossipy person could have inferred a lot about his or her neighbors by doing so. Once the librarians realized this problem, they moved the hold items behind the desk so that patrons had to request access to them.

If patrons thought that librarians (or others, such as nosy neighbors, law enforcement, or government officials) were monitoring their reading, that would change some of their reading habits. This, in turn, would impinge on the freedom to explore and freedom of thought.

Consider the classic example of exploring presidential assassination attempts. Why might a person want to know details about assassinations? Why study murder and attempted murder of our elected leaders? Surely, there are many possible answers to these questions, most of which are quite innocent and simple.

Ard (2013) explains that library norms and professional ethics, as well as state law, generally ensure privacy for library records. While there is no federal law protecting the confidentiality of library records, forty-eight states (and the District of Columbia) have laws protecting the confidentiality of library records; the remaining two states have opinions by their attorneys general supporting library record confidentiality (ALA, 2007b).

In an interpretation of the Library Bill of Rights, the ALA states that "privacy is essential to the exercise of free speech, free thought, and free association" (ALA, 2006d, para. 1). This ties privacy ineluctably to freedom to explore. We need privacy to pursue our thoughts and dreams, as well as to explore new ones. The ALA statement also adds, "The right to privacy is the right to open inquiry without having the subject of one's interest examined or scrutinized by others" (para. 2).

Another example comes from writers; there is a well-known cliché about the search terms of authors, especially mystery writers. An author might explore deadly poison, asphyxiation, hiding a body, and so on. If a suspicious person examined the writer's search terms, he or she could conclude that the writer was plotting an actual murder instead of trying to write the next bestseller. Instead, the writer needs privacy to utilize the freedom to explore however and whatever he or she wishes. Privacy carves out space to utilize the freedom to explore without judgment or insinuations.

CONCLUSION

In this chapter, we have explored the freedom to explore and its connection to intellectual freedom. The freedom to explore is a unique and valuable way to think about the exploring that our patrons can do in our libraries. They may consider many different perspectives for information and learning or for pleasure and recreation. Patrons can also conduct thought experiments through the freedom to explore and the wide diversity of views available in libraries, thinking through different perspectives and options. Central to the freedom to explore is privacy. This principle gives people protection while they are exploring, freeing them from others' potential judgment.

REFERENCES

American Library Association. (2006a). Diversity in collection development: An interpretation of the library bill of rights. Retrieved from http://www.ala.org/advocacy/intfreedom/librarybill/interpretations/ diversitycollection. Document ID: 73f91c8d-ec1c-1e24-7d16-910de 935ad33.

American Library Association. (2006b). Freedom to read statement. Retrieved from http://www.ala.org/advocacy/intfreedom/freedom readstatement. Document ID: aaac95d4-2988-0024-6573-10a5ce 6b21b2.

American Library Association. (2006c). Library bill of rights. Retrieved from http://www.ala.org/advocacy/intfreedom/librarybill. Document ID: 669fd6a3-8939-3e54-7577-996a0a3f8952.

American Library Association. (2006d). Privacy: An interpretation of the Library Bill of Rights. Retrieved from http://www.ala.org/ advocacy/intfreedom/librarybill/interpretations/privacy. Document ID: 5c653c23-920b-b254-d94c-6dcf4ccd86c6.

American Library Association. (2007a). Intellectual freedom and censorship Q&A. Retrieved from http://www.ala.org/advocacy/intfreedom/ censorship/faq. Document ID: e8ae9ed7-a469-f0d4-adf0-f2770d2ca8e8.

American Library Association. (2007b). State privacy laws regarding library records. Retrieved from http://www.ala.org/advocacy/privacy/statelaws. Document ID: 059bd305-beb0-3a34-5967-c7b5e66dff2f.

American Library Association. (2009). Advocating for intellectual freedom: An interpretation of the library bill of rights. Retrieved from http://www.ala.org/advocacy/intfreedom/librarybill/interpretations/advocating-intellectual-freedom. Document ID: fd641f16-d02e-17c4-d545-95d1258a622c.

American Library Association. (2017). Politics in American libraries: An interpretation of the library bill of rights. Retrieved from http://www.ala.org/advocacy/intfreedom/librarybill/interpretations/politics. Document ID: 7ad4ea0e-894f-c224-b907-38c1a94e7fbf.

Ard, B.J. (2013). Confidentiality and the problem of third parties: Protecting reader privacy in the age of intermediaries. *Yale Journal of Law & Technology, 16*(1), 1–58.

Blitz, M.J. (2006). Constitutional safeguards for silent experiments in living: Libraries, the right to read, and a First Amendment theory for an unaccompanied right to receive information. *University of Missouri–Kansas City Law Review, 74*(4), 799–882.

Foucault, M. (1991). *Discipline and punish: The birth of the prison.* London, England: Penguin.

Kennedy, B.M. (1989). Confidentiality of library records: A survey of problems, policies, and laws. *Law Library Journal, 81*(4), 733–768.

Richards, N. (2008). Intellectual privacy. *Texas Law Review, 87*(2), 387–446.

Robertson, E. (2011). A fundamental right to read: Reader privacy protections in the U.S. Constitution. *University of Colorado Law Review, 82*(1), 307–330.

Stanley v. Georgia, 394 U.S. 557 (1969).

United States v. Rumely, 345 U.S. 41 (1953).

FOUR

Core Values and Intellectual Freedom

Core values are essential attributes of an organization or a profession—the central beliefs about how and why an institution does what it does. Former American Library Association's (ALA) president Michael Gorman (2000) wrote that values are

> standards by which we can assess what we do; measure how near we are to, or how far we are from, an objective; and compare our actions and our state of being to those of others and to the ideals represented by our values. (p. 7)

In other words, values can be a useful yardstick to gauge action and determine whether the action matches the goals and vision of an institution. In our discussion, we are focused on whether certain actions on behalf of a library match the ideals of librarianship. Core values are useful ways to consider these ideals and how to put them into action.

The ALA defined librarianship's core values in 2006, stating that these eleven principles are the "essential set of core values that define, inform, and guide our professional practice" (ALA, 2006a); the values are access, confidentiality/privacy, democracy, diversity, education and lifelong learning, intellectual freedom, preservation, the public good, professionalism, service, and social responsibility. As you can see, intellectual freedom is one of the core values of the profession.

The other ten core values are either served by or operate in service to intellectual freedom. This means that intellectual freedom gives strength and support to many of the other core values, and they reciprocally do the same for intellectual freedom. This is explained and expanded upon in the sections that follow.

INTELLECTUAL FREEDOM AS A CORE VALUE

First, we start by discussing intellectual freedom as a core value. The ALA defines intellectual freedom as

> the right of every individual to both seek and receive information from all points of view without restriction. It provides for free access to all expressions of ideas through which any and all sides of a question, cause or movement may be explored. (ALA, 2007a, para. 1)

In Chapter 1, we discussed the First Amendment and the fact that freedom of speech includes the right to seek (or receive) information (see also Oltmann, 2016). Thus, intellectual freedom is a part of freedom of speech and is protected by the First Amendment. This gives strong legal protection to intellectual freedom in the United States.

It is important to note that intellectual freedom includes not just seeking information but also seeking access to "any and all sides." *Any* perspective is fair game from an intellectual freedom point of view. For libraries, this broad conception has consequences: it means we must try to accommodate access to as many perspectives as we can.

Perhaps your library has resources arguing about the dangers of contact sports like football and hockey along with resources that have different perspectives (suggesting the dangers are mitigated or that players are freely choosing to expose themselves to the dangers). Another option is to allow unrestricted access to the internet for your patrons. There are many ways to facilitate access to "any and all" perspectives, and libraries have a duty to do so.

Arguably, intellectual freedom—providing free access to all expressions— is the core mission of most libraries. This applies to libraries of all types (public, school, academic, and special libraries) to varying degrees. As Chapter 5 discusses, each type of library has a unique community that it serves. For its particular community, the library's goal is usually broad access.

Because intellectual freedom is so central to libraries, we can consider how each of the other ten core values (listed earlier) relates to intellectual freedom. This will help demonstrate the foundational importance of intellectual freedom as well as reiterate its importance to libraries.

ACCESS

In the *ALA Policy Manual*, access is defined as "all information resources that are provided directly or indirectly by the library, regardless of technology, format, or methods of delivery, should be readily, equally, and equitably accessible to all library users" (found at http://www.ala.org/aboutala/governance/policymanual/updatedpolicymanual/section2/53intellfreedom#B.2.1.15). Here, we can see that access in librarianship emphasizes the *equity* of access to all users and across all formats.

Gorman (2015) echoes this emphasis: "We must begin with the basic premise that everyone has a right to have access to library resources and services, irrespective of who they are and where and under which conditions they live" (p. 159). Thus, characteristics like gender, age, race/ethnicity, economic status, sexual orientation, and national origin should not affect an individual's access rights. This is in contrast to years past. Public libraries, like many institutions, used to be segregated. Some libraries shut down rather than become integrated (Knott, 2015).

Individual Characteristics and Access

While people of color generally do not face such *overt* barriers today, there may still be subtle barriers to their full access and involvement in libraries. Are the locations and hours of operations convenient for all populations in your community? Are materials that might particularly appeal to people of color collected? Are there items in different languages (e.g., Spanish for Hispanic users)? Are there staff members who speak different languages? Is programming offered at varying times in varying languages?

Not every question here needs to be answered "yes" for every library, but these sorts of questions should regularly be considered, as demographics change and populations fluctuate. If your library does not know whether these questions would be important for your community, then research needs to be done.

Age is another important characteristic to consider, though it is one that is particularly controversial in public and school libraries. The ALA's official stance is that access to information should not be curtailed because of someone's age. The fifth principle of the Library Bill of Rights says, "A person's right to use a library should not be denied or abridged because of origin, *age*, background, or views" (ALA, 2006b, para. 6, emphasis added).

This is a simple and explicit directive. It means that if your library has R-rated movies, anyone should be allowed to check them out, even minors (unless state law forbids it). Minors should have access to the full range of materials in a library, even salacious books, music, or videos. It is *not* a librarian's job to restrict access; it *is* a librarian's job to enable access.

Rather than banning access, librarians can try to redirect youth to more appropriate materials. Librarians can, and should, rely on parents and guardians to guide their children to materials that the adults view as appropriate (this is what the ALA suggests). Many people also note that children may want to check out a salacious book but then quickly lose interest as the story and vocabulary go over their head. This issue becomes a bit more complicated in school libraries, where educators (and librarians) act in loco parentis and have responsibility for the minors in their care. (See Chapter 5 for more on this.)

Other Potential Barriers to Access

Beyond individual characteristics such as race/ethnicity and age, we need to think more broadly about potential barriers to access and do whatever we can to eliminate or reduce them. This is the central meaning behind "access" as a core value of librarianship.

Fines for overdue books can become one such barrier. For many years, most libraries have charged fines when patrons return books late, and generally libraries have cut off access to library resources once the fines accumulate to a certain point (e.g., a $25 maximum). For people in lower economic status, however, such a temporary restriction can end up being tantamount to a permanent restriction, because even this small amount is too large to pay. This can be exacerbated when adults have large fines and blocked access, resulting in reduced or no access for their children.

Libraries have begun to recognize that overdue fines can inadvertently result in reduced access for some patrons. In many libraries, when fines accumulate to a certain amount, borrowing privileges are suspended. For many patrons, especially those from low socioeconomic backgrounds, paying down fines is not within their budget—hence, they are essentially no longer able to check out materials.

As a result, many libraries are now doing away with fines. Some libraries have programs where patrons can "read off" their fines or bring in canned goods or other donations to reduce their fines. Other libraries have simply eliminated fines altogether (Fenske, 2018; Graham, 2017; Wenger, 2018).

Other potential barriers include physical impediments, such as narrow aisles, lack of elevator or ramps, shelves too low or too high, or no computers with wheelchair-accessible desks. Thinking about and rectifying physical barriers help those with disabilities, the elderly, and the very young. It also aids those with invisible disabilities (e.g., chronic illnesses).

A final potential barrier to access has to do with hours of operation and scheduling events or programming. Many public libraries schedule storytime on a weekday morning, but this then limits access to those families who have a stay-at-home parent, nanny, or similar situation. Families in which both parents work and the children go to daycare are probably not going to be able to take advantage of such a storytime. And we know from research that this will disproportionately affect those from lower socioeconomic conditions and people of color. Thus, scheduling storytime during the weekday can inadvertently affect access for marginalized groups.

A similar problem happens with programming scheduled during the day, such as an afternoon book club. You may get many retirees to attend but few adults of working age. Again, this may disproportionately affect people of color and lower socioeconomic status. This holds true for other types of libraries as well. Academic libraries that hold programming events during the day may get some types of students but not others (often, not students who have to work while attending college).

Hours of operation, likewise, can end up reducing or preventing access for some groups in your community. Whenever possible, hours in the evening and on the weekend are a good idea to expand access to more people. You may see different segments of your community frequent the library if you adjust the hours.

This value of access ties in closely to intellectual freedom. The concept of intellectual freedom supports this core value of access by positioning access as a right guaranteed by the First Amendment (see Chapter 1). This strengthens the importance of access. In turn, the core value of access serves intellectual freedom by ensuring patrons can gain entry to a wide range of views and perspectives. Thinking about *access*, specifically, can help remove potential barriers that might limit intellectual freedom. Access and intellectual freedom are closely entwined.

CONFIDENTIALITY/PRIVACY

The second core value listed by the ALA is confidentiality and privacy, which the organization describes as "fundamental to the ethics and practices of librarianship" (ALA, 2006a, para. 4). A great deal has been written to define these concepts (e.g., Solove, 2002, 2005). Here, we rely on a general understanding that privacy is the freedom to seek information without being scrutinized or judged (see ALA, 2007b). Again, Gorman (2015) has an interesting take on this: "Much of the relationship between a library and its patrons is based on trust, and, in a free society, a library user should be secure in trusting us" to not reveal personal information, including which resources are being used by whom (p. 185).

Chapter 3 discussed the importance of privacy to the freedom of thought. If someone believes he or she is being monitored, he or she will curtail his or her actions in various ways. Thus, a right to privacy allows us to be fully free to explore any thought that crosses our mind. It is important to note that privacy is important for all aspects of intellectual freedom, including seeking, receiving, and using information.

Intellectual freedom is heightened by privacy: the core value of privacy enables one to fully utilize intellectual freedom. For example, a classic example of the intersection between privacy and intellectual freedom arises in the reference interview. Imagine a young adult comes to the desk, seeking information about teen pregnancy or coming out as lesbian, gay, or bisexual. (This sort of interaction has occurred in school, public, and academic libraries.) These are potentially inflammatory issues for which the patron likely expects (or *trusts*) that there will be privacy.

It is only this assumption of privacy that allows the patron to exercise his or her intellectual freedom in seeking new information. If the information request was going to be shared with parents, classmates, other staff members, or the entire community, the intellectual freedom to seek such information would be shattered. Thus, privacy is truly an essential condition for intellectual freedom.

DEMOCRACY

Democracy is another topic about which much has been written, trying to define and describe it, but a general understanding of this form of governance as it exists in the United States is sufficient for our discussion.

The ALA notes that "a democracy presupposes an informed citizenry" (ALA, 2006a, para. 5). In a democracy organized like the United States, eligible voters are supposed to cast votes for the people who best represent their views and then hold the representatives accountable (through letter writing, phone calls, protests, and voting in the future for a different candidate, if the first one is not an accurate representative).

Both of these aspects—voting for the most-representative candidate and holding the representative accountable—require people to be informed. Citizens must be informed about political platforms, key issues, the wider sociopolitical context, the economy, the stances and actions of representatives, and the overall system of governance (i.e., how the three branches of government work together).

This is quite a responsibility, and in our modern society, it can be quite difficult; in fact, many people choose (or seem to choose) to be not well informed (Delli Carpini, Cook, & Jacobs, 2004). It is even more difficult in our age of fake news, suspicion of the media, and social media rumors (Mitchell, Gottfried, Barthel, & Sumida, 2018). Nonetheless, the *ideal* is an informed citizenry, and for this, we need intellectual freedom.

Intellectual freedom helps bolster democratic ideals and goals by providing and protecting access to a wide range of ideas. Recall that intellectual freedom provides access for "any and all sides" to a question or an issue.

Imagine someone wants to vote for candidates who stand for the best health care for the widest range of people. To do so, this person would have to understand various healthcare plans, such as universal care and private insurance; evaluate the advantages and disadvantages of these options; and investigate the stance of multiple candidates.

Intellectual freedom would enable this intellectual exploration. Even if universal health care were an unpopular perspective in this person's community, he or she would still be able to explore it to learn more, make a determination, and decide whom to support in upcoming elections. This is the principle of democracy in action, enabled by intellectual freedom.

DIVERSITY

The ALA does not define diversity, which can be understood in many different ways. Cooke (2017) defines diversity as the "state or fact of being diverse; different characteristics and experiences that define individuals" (p. 7).

The ALA emphasizes that "we value our nation's diversity and strive to reflect that diversity by providing a full spectrum of resources and services to the communities we serve" (ALA, 2006a, para. 7). Without naming every single attribute or characteristic that is important to people (e.g., race/ethnicity or economic status), we can celebrate all dimensions of diversity—the full spectrum of diversity, as the statement says.

For the ALA, the focus is on providing resources and services to communities. This includes not only resources that reflect one's local community but also resources that go beyond and showcase the broader humanity of all communities.

Even if you live in a geographical area that is fairly homogenous, you can (and should) offer a wide range of resources that illustrate the wonderful diversity of society, which can spark curiosity and compassion for others. For example, some rural areas have little racial or ethnic diversity (though that is often changing), but libraries in these areas should nonetheless select books and other resources that reflect a variety of lived experiences—those of immigrants, nonwhite residents, urban and suburban dwellers, and a variety of backgrounds and careers.

Some residents of these areas will leave and travel to new places (migrating to urban areas for education and jobs, for example). Some residents will marry or befriend people who are different from them. Some residents will enjoy learning about people different from themselves. All will benefit from having the opportunity to do so.

Diverse library materials act as both a *window* and a *mirror* for patrons of all types of libraries (Bishop, 1990; Glazier & Seo, 2005; Smolkin & Young, 2011). As a mirror, diverse library materials allow people from diverse communities to see themselves reflected in what they are reading. For example, LGBT youth often suffer from anxiety regarding their sexuality and acceptance by friends and family; reading about teens with similar experiences can provide support and encouragement. This creates opportunities for individuals to reflect on their own experiences, often gaining more self-awareness and understanding. It allows people to see themselves as part of the world (Oltmann, 2017).

Diverse literature serves as a window when it allows insight into the experiences of others. White individuals, for instance, may learn about the perspectives and situations of people of color, increasing understanding and empathy. Those who are not members of multicultural or marginalized groups can benefit, as diverse books help them "understand and respect differences and diversity" (Loh, 2006, p. 46). Naidoo (2014) emphasizes that multicultural resources provide "the opportunity to learn how to function in a culturally pluralistic world" (p. 6).

The principles of intellectual freedom can help further the cause of diversity. Because an intellectual freedom perspective defends having multiple points of view on every topic, this creates room for diverse viewpoints. This can include different political perspectives, for instance, or different sociocultural views. For example, your library may have books touting various diet regimes and other books that caution against any diet. Or a library may have books both critical of and sympathetic to the Black Lives Matter movement, as well as the full spectrum in between these stances.

EDUCATION AND LIFELONG LEARNING

Another core value of librarianship is lifelong learning. The ALA encourages "the creation, maintenance, and enhancement of a learning society" through collaboration with educators, government officials, parents, organizations, and others who can contribute to this goal (ALA, 2006a, para. 7).

A learning society is often seen as a key component for success (for both individuals and societies) in the modern technological age because it promotes ongoing learning and development. It is easy to see how libraries of all kinds can fit into this vision, as they provide the resources, tools, and programming to create, perpetuate, and inspire lifelong learning.

Intellectual freedom supports lifelong learning just as it strengthens other values. True learning happens when we encounter new information or a different perspective on what we already know. This can only happen, of course, when there are a variety of perspectives available—the more diverse the information, and the more diverse the sources of that information, the better chances that we can learn from it. As we have seen, intellectual freedom allows for this possibility.

Climate change serves as an excellent example for both the importance of lifelong learning and the importance of providing a wealth of information. Scientists continually update our knowledge about climate change and its effects on rising sea levels, endangered animals, and natural disasters; significant information comes from around the world. A library dedicated to lifelong learning must seek to include the latest and most valuable information on climate change so that its patrons can learn about this phenomenon and what can be done.

At the same time, an orientation toward lifelong learning will often serve to strengthen support for intellectual freedom. If an individual believes strongly in lifelong learning, by implication he or she also believes in the importance of having new and different information available. Scientists by nature tend to be curious learners. In our example about climate change earlier, these scientists would advocate for new, emerging information about climate change's effects to be widely shared and made available.

THE PUBLIC GOOD

As part of its explanation of this core value, the ALA states that "libraries are an essential public good and are fundamental institutions in democratic societies" (ALA, 2006a, para. 9). The "public good" means a resource or service that, fundamentally, serves the public well-being.

In an economic sense, a public good is nonexcludable and nonrivalrous; this means that people cannot really be excluded from using it. If one person uses it, another person (a "rival" in economics) can still use it. (In contrast, a country club would be considered excludable because people can be blocked from using it, and a steak would be a rivalrous good, because if one person consumes it, no one else can.)

Some types of school, academic, and special libraries may not be completely nonexcludable, as they have restrictions on who is counted as a patron, but within their patron base, libraries generally allow all to use their resources. And most library resources (with the exception of some e-resources like licensed books) are nonrivalrous: one person "consuming" a book or a movie does not stop others from likewise consuming it.

Beyond an Economic Argument

However, an economic definition is not necessary to understand the argument of the ALA. Their basic stance is that libraries exist to benefit the public. This is a very strong statement defending libraries' value to our society.

This is true of all types of libraries. The argument may be easiest to see for public libraries, which do literally serve the public community. School libraries serve students, staff, and teachers, often helping enhance literacy and preparing students to be engaged, productive members of society. Academic libraries similarly prepare college students—and enable faculty members to produce scholarship to better society. Special libraries, in their own unique ways, benefit their users and often help them give back to society (as seen in, for example, hospital or law libraries).

Of course, one way that libraries serve the public is through intellectual freedom. Having a wide range of perspectives available, and defending the decision to do so, is essential to serving one's community well (see the sections on "Diversity" and "Democracy"). When a diversity of viewpoints is available, an individual is more likely to find something that sounds interesting, relevant, or useful to him or her.

PRESERVATION

The ALA explains that "the Association supports the preservation of information published in all media and formats. The association [*sic*] affirms that the preservation of information resources is central to libraries and librarianship" (ALA, 2006a, para. 10). Preservation, of course, is often the focus of archivists and special libraries, with their own unique perspectives and areas of emphasis. Nonetheless, virtually all libraries utilize this core value in some way, even if it is primarily preserving or maintaining resources that are well-used by the community.

While it may at first be difficult to see the relationship between preservation and intellectual freedom, preservation is, in fact, quite important for maintaining intellectual freedom. A diversity of viewpoints does not usually spring up all at once but generally accumulates over time, often centuries. We need to preserve earlier works (in diverse formats) so that current and future generations can access them. Poetry from the ancient Greeks, for example, is found in many formats and has been preserved as well as possible; it still informs and shapes poetry written today.

Items that are "born digital" may be of special concern in this respect. These items never existed on paper but only in electronic forms. As software gets updated, styles change, and formats evolve, earlier digital resources may no longer be accessible. In addition, digital data can be corrupted as they are updated and transferred, leading to subtle changes in documents. Yet the early years of the internet age were transformative and contain information and data that could be valuable in our contemporary age. This is an important preservation problem with clear intellectual freedom implications.

Another related preservation concern is which items get preserved and which get destroyed. Historically, few preservation efforts have been focused on the voices of the marginalized, the dispossessed, and the disenfranchised; for example, relatively few examples of letters written by African Americans in the eighteenth and nineteenth centuries still exist today, because efforts were not made to preserve them (see Shapiro, 2017, for a counterexample). At the time, these were not considered important documents about important people, so little care was taken to preserve them.

In the past few decades, however, the archives and preservation fields have become much more cognizant of this shortcoming and have worked to rectify this imbalance. This will help to preserve *all* voices for the future, ensuring more perspectives are available (and enabling stronger intellectual diversity).

PROFESSIONALISM

Professionalism involves how we are educated and trained and how we serve our patrons. The ALA says,

> The American Library Association supports the provision of library services by professionally qualified personnel who have been educated in graduate programs within institutions of higher education. It is of vital importance that there be professional education available to meet the social needs and goals of library services. (ALA, 2006a, para. 11)

Professional, graduate-level education is an important way that librarians learn about these core values, professional ethics, and the theoretical foundations that undergird the day-to-day practices of libraries.

Yet professionalism goes beyond formal education. It can be seen in the way we provide patron services (e.g., readers' advisory, programming, computer assistance). Do we offer consistently equal and equitable service to all patrons, regardless of age, race/ethnicity, gender, sexual orientation, or ability?

Assisting individuals with computers, for example, can be tedious and frustrating, but we should not allow patrons' lack of technological competency to result in less-than-professional service. Similarly, crying children and irritated parents need to be met with calm compassion and professional service.

Our colleagues deserve the same levels of respect and understanding as well. We should be kind to one another, especially if we are encountering difficult patrons or a rough day. The ALA Code of Ethics' fifth principle is "we treat co-workers and other colleagues with respect, fairness, and good faith, and advocate conditions of employment that safeguard the rights and welfare of all employees of our institutions" (ALA, 2017, principle 5).

Another aspect of professionalism is the ability to set aside one's personal beliefs and preferences while at work. For example, one person may have strong religious beliefs that include dismissing all other religions as false paths. As a librarian, however, this person must set aside his or her personal beliefs and serve all patrons competently, regardless of the religion of the patron or the information the patron is seeking.

The librarian cannot pass judgment or condemn the information that is sought but should instead help this patron in the same manner as any other patron. If all patrons are treated equitably and assisted competently, then we are helping them to enact intellectual freedom. There will be an absence of barriers hindering information access.

In addition, professionalism can be foundational for carrying out intellectual freedom in the library. As discussed in Chapter 7, every library should have a collection development (CD) policy, and every CD policy should contain a section on intellectual freedom. This can demonstrate to one's community that intellectual freedom is a core value of the profession, not just a whim of a particular person.

SERVICE

Closely related to professionalism, service is one of the core values that should guide librarians daily. The ALA states, "We strive for excellence in the profession by maintaining and enhancing our own knowledge and skills, by encouraging the professional development of co-workers, and by fostering the aspirations of potential members of the profession" (ALA, 2006a, para. 12).

This quotation is taken directly from the ALA Code of Ethics (ALA, 2017); because it is part of both the Core Values and the Code of Ethics, the importance of service cannot be overlooked. Most librarians realize this; for example, in a survey of school librarians, over 94 percent replied that "service" was very important in their libraries (Oltmann, 2018).

Service is not an abstract lofty ideal but the nitty-gritty of how we interact with our patrons day after day. It includes "other duties as assigned," that nebulous phrase that encompasses so much in the life of a library (often including duties that no one likes to do, such as bathroom cleanup). Service can also be seen in the librarian who goes the extra mile to find a patron's desired information or to help a patron use the computer effectively (Arnett, 2018; Wilkins Jordan, 2014).

When we defend and enact intellectual freedom, we are, ultimately, serving our patrons. The concept of intellectual freedom exists so that our patrons have the freedom to explore ideas and access information. Having a strong intellectual freedom mind-set and policy means that we can provide a wide range of perspectives, better serving diverse patrons.

SOCIAL RESPONSIBILITY

The final core value of librarianship, according to the ALA, is social responsibility. This entails a responsibility to society, to "ameliorating or solving the critical problems of society" and enabling individuals and groups to become educated and to solve these problems themselves (ALA, 2006a, para. 12).

Social responsibility is a concept that has received increasing attention in the past thirty years, moving into the mainstream. The idea is that we are not alone but are all a part of the broader society. The large societal problems we face (e.g., generational poverty or institutional racism) can only be tackled if we work together and bring our social institutions together to collaborate on solving these issues.

Libraries can contribute to social responsibility in several ways. One of the most significant things that libraries can do is provide opportunities for education, reflection, learning, and growth (see Chapter 3 for a discussion on the freedom to explore, which is closely related).

An individual could learn about generational poverty, for example, by growing up in an affected household or through careful observation of one's community, but to view this phenomenon systematically and in an integrated fashion, additional learning will probably be necessary. Libraries can offer the books and other resources to fulfill this. Individuals can learn about societal factors that contribute to either the problem or the solutions.

In addition, libraries can be places where communities come together to address large, seemingly intractable problems. Perhaps a special speaker or programming event can help inform and unite people to address such issues. Libraries can also position themselves as part of the solution to societal issues; this holds true for all types of libraries located in different types of communities.

Social responsibility, ultimately, is about working together to address societal wrongs and make things better for and within our diverse society. Intellectual freedom has a clear role to play here. It is needed to ensure that a wide range of perspectives is available; resources that identify and describe societal problems, propose resolutions and strategies, and address collaboration and communication are all needed.

CONCLUSION

In this chapter, we have discussed how each of the core values of librarianship is connected with intellectual freedom. The core values are access, confidentiality/privacy, democracy, diversity, education and lifelong learning, intellectual freedom, preservation, the public good, professionalism, service, and social responsibility.

Each of these core values enhances intellectual freedom in some way and is strengthened when a library practices strong intellectual freedom. The core values, in this way, mutually reinforce one another. Because intellectual freedom is so central to the core mission of most libraries, it can be seen as the thread that ties all of the core values together.

REFERENCES

American Library Association. (2006a). Core values of librarianship. Retrieved from http://www.ala.org/advocacy/intfreedom/corevalues. Document ID: 33390955-19b0-2164-9d0d-07dfe5ec504e.

American Library Association. (2006b). Library bill of rights. Retrieved from http://www.ala.org/advocacy/intfreedom/librarybill. Document ID: 669fd6a3-8939-3e54-7577-996a0a3f8952.

American Library Association. (2007a). Intellectual freedom and censorship Q&A. Retrieved from http://www.ala.org/advocacy/intfreedom/censorship/faq. Document ID: e8ae9ed7-a469-f0d4-adf0-f2770d2ca8e8.

American Library Association. (2007b). Questions and answers on privacy and confidentiality. Retrieved from http://www.ala.org/advocacy/privacy/FAQ. Document ID: 748167ea-002c-2d74-05c8-ed4ad9dd4715.

American Library Association. (2017). Professional ethics. Retrieved from http://www.ala.org/tools/ethics. Document ID: 39f580a8-833d-5ad4-f900-53ecfe67eb1f.

Arnett, K. (2018). What exactly does a librarian do? Everything. Lit Hub. Retrieved from https://lithub.com/what-exactly-does-a-librarian-do-everything/

Bishop, R. S. (1990). Mirrors, windows, and sliding glass doors. *Perspectives: Choosing and Using Books for the Classroom, 6*(1), 9–11.

Cooke, N. A. (2017). *Information services to diverse populations: Developing culturally competent library professionals.* Santa Barbara, CA: Libraries Unlimited.

Delli Carpini, M. X., Cook, F. L., & Jacobs, L. R. (2004). Public deliberation, discursive participation, and citizen engagement: A review of the empirical literature. *Annual Review of Political Science, 7,* 315–344.

Fenske, S. (2018). The St. Louis Public Library is no longer charging daily overdue fines. *Riverfront Times.* Retrieved from https://www.

riverfronttimes.com/newsblog/2018/10/18/the-st-louis-public-library-is-no-longer-charging-overdue-fines

Glazier, J., & Seo, J.-A. (2005). Multicultural literature and discussion as mirror and window? *Journal of Adolescent & Adult Literacy, 48*(8), 686–700.

Gorman, M. (2000). *Our enduring values: Librarianship in the 21st century.* Chicago, IL: American Library Association.

Gorman, M. (2015). *Our enduring values revisited: Librarianship in an ever-changing world.* Chicago, IL: American Library Association.

Graham, R. (2017). Long overdue: Why public libraries are finally eliminating the late-return fine. *Slate.* Retrieved from http://www.slate.com/articles/arts/culturebox/2017/02/librarians_are_realizing_that_overdue_fines_undercut_libraries_missions.html

Knott, C. (2015). *Not free, not for all: Public libraries in the age of Jim Crow.* Amherst, MA: University of Massachusetts Press.

Loh, V. (2006). Quantity and quality: The need for culturally authentic trade books in Asian-American young adult literature. *The ALAN Review, 34*(1), 44–61.

Mitchell, A., Gottfried, J., Barthel, M., & Sumida, N. (2018). Distinguishing between factual and opinion statements in the news. Pew Research Center. Retrieved from http://www.journalism.org/2018/06/18/distinguishing-between-factual-and-opinion-statements-in-the-news/

Naidoo, J.C. (2014). The importance of diversity in library programs and material collections for children. Association for Library Service to Children (ALSC) White Paper. Retrieved from http://www.ala.org/alsc/sites/ala.org.alsc/files/content/ALSCwhitepaper_importance%20of%20diversity_with%20graphics_FINAL.pdf

Oltmann, S.M. (2016). Intellectual freedom and freedom of speech: Three theoretical perspectives. *Library Quarterly, 86*(2), 153–171.

Oltmann, S.M. (2017). Creating space at the table: Intellectual freedom can bolster diverse voices. *Library Quarterly, 87*(4), 410–418.

Oltmann, S.M. (2018). Ethics, values, and intellectual freedom in school libraries. *School Libraries Worldwide, 24*(1), 71–86.

Shapiro, A. (2017). After slavery, searching for loved ones in wanted ads. *NPR Code Switch.* Retrieved from https://www.npr.org/sections/codeswitch/2017/02/22/516651689/after-slavery-searching-for-loved-ones-in-wanted-ads

Smolkin, L.B., & Young, C.A. (2011). Missing mirrors, missing windows: Children's literature textbooks and LGBT topics. *Language Arts, 88*(3), 217–225.

Solove, D.J. (2002). Conceptualizing privacy. *California Law Review, 90*(4), 1087–1155.

Solove, D.J. (2005). A taxonomy of privacy. *University of Pennsylvania Law Review, 154*(3), 477–564.

Wenger, Y. (2018). Baltimore's Pratt Library goes fine free for overdue books. *The Baltimore Sun.* Retrieved from http://www.baltimoresun.com/news/maryland/baltimore-city/bs-md-ci-pratt-fine-free-20180518-story.html

Wilkins Jordan, M. (2014). Reference desks in public libraries: What happens and what to know. *Reference Librarian, 55*(3), 196–211. Retrieved from https://www-tandfonline-com.ezproxy.uky.edu/doi/full/10.1080/02763877.2014.910742

FIVE

Intellectual Freedom in the Daily Lives of Libraries

In the first four chapters, this book articulated the theoretical and philosophical foundations of intellectual freedom. With that basis, we can turn now to the ways that intellectual freedom impacts the daily activities and operations of different types of libraries. While the case for intellectual freedom may be strongest for public libraries, it is an important, foundational value for all types of libraries.

Each type of library has a unique community it serves. In sociology, a community is often understood to be as "a group of persons (a) engaging in social interaction, (b) within a geographic area, and (c) having a common tie or ties" (Goe & Noonan, 2006, p. 457). Communities, however, do not have to be geographically bound, especially with the rise of the information society and the connective capabilities of the internet.

For public libraries, the community is generally the town or city in which the library is located—usually everyone within a limited geographical area. Some libraries may have reciprocal agreements with surrounding counties or communities, which expands the service area somewhat.

Other types of libraries still have a "community" they serve, even if their patron base is not grounded in a geographical understanding of com munity. For example, a school library serves its community of students, teachers, and staff (and sometimes parents or others affiliated with the school). Academic libraries usually serve people affiliated with their institution, though it may be expanded to include people in the geographical community as well (especially for institutions funded with public tax dollars). Finally, special libraries tend to have the most restricted patron bases. Usually these are based on the type of materials in the collection and who might need access to them. Hospital libraries, for example, typically serve hospital patients, their families, and medical staff.

From an intellectual freedom perspective, the community that is served is an important consideration. The intellectual freedom concerns and challenges will, in large part, be driven by the particular communities in question, as the rest of the chapter describes.

PUBLIC LIBRARIES

In some respects, public libraries have the broadest patron base—usually everyone in a particular geographical area. This makes intellectual freedom concerns both very simple and very broad. On one hand, public libraries do not have to consider specialized populations—everyone (at least in theory) is subject to the same policies and approaches. On the other hand, this means that the policies must be well-thought-out and defended strongly, since they are applicable to everyone.

Minors in the Public Library

Many public libraries struggle to apply the same policy equitably to all patrons, particularly minors; unfortunately, minors' rights to information access are often curtailed under the guise of "protecting" them from potentially controversial or sensitive information. This could include information about puberty/developing bodies; LGBT content; information about various religious beliefs (including atheism); books about wizards, magic, and other fantasy elements; or anything with sexual information or connotation. Most of the frequently challenged books, as noted by the American Library Association's (ALA) Office for Intellectual Freedom, are geared toward minors and include some of the content described previously (ALA, 2013).

The Supreme Court has carefully considered minors' First Amendment rights and has concluded that minors enjoy nearly the same broad range of freedom as adults, only slightly limited. This means, in effect, that concern about exposing minors to certain content is often misplaced: most content is legally protected, and minors have a right to access it. The difficulty lies in explaining this to community members, especially those concerned about minors, such as parents, guardians, and grandparents.

In addition, it is important to remember that many minors do not come from ideal homes; they often face difficult circumstances in their own lives. For example, a teen may have a parent suffering from addiction or financial insecurity. Reading about similar characters and situations may make them feel less alone and give them comfort. Youth may have parents going through divorce. Thus, realistic fiction (especially for teens) can serve a valuable purpose.

The approach recommended by the ALA is to encourage parents and guardians to supervise what their children check out and what their children access; rather than making the library responsible for *all* minors, this approach makes each family unit responsible for their particular minors. It means that a broad range of information is still available for others who may desire it.

Similarly, the ALA discourages restricting children's access to certain ranges of books (e.g., preventing teens from checking out books in the adult section). Minors have a wide range of reading ability, interest level, and curiosity, and public libraries should not participate in dampening those features.

Again, if parents want to restrict their own (and only their own) children, that is a different, reasonable approach. Restricting access more broadly would impact too many people, and since a public library, by its very definition, serves the general public, that would be unfair.

Internet Filtering

Public libraries must also think carefully about internet filtering (see Chapter 10). On one hand, applying internet filtering means that libraries would be eligible for certain federal funding programs that greatly reduce the cost of providing internet access.

On the other hand, applying internet filtering means restricting access to a broad swathe of people—everyone—since filters must be deployed on all computers to become eligible for the funding. In a time of budget cuts, this can be a very difficult decision to make.

Ideally, the library's board of trustees would be fully informed about the advantages and disadvantages of filtering and then make a careful decision. From an intellectual freedom perspective, of course, internet filtering is highly problematic because it often restricts access to needed, valuable information that is protected by the First Amendment.

Other Intellectual Freedom Concerns

In addition to these concerns, public libraries have a number of other intellectual freedom concerns, such as meeting rooms, collection development policies, displays, and programming. (Part II of this book will address these concerns in more detail.) Most types of libraries share some of these concerns, but they are often most prominent in public libraries.

Public libraries should also be thoughtful and careful about the patron records that they create and store. For example, how long are circulation records kept? Some libraries keep these records indefinitely, while other libraries keep only the most recent transaction. Similarly, many libraries destroy records of reference questions, computer room or programming sign-up sheets, computer logs, and so on.

These moves are made to protect patron privacy from law enforcement searches (see Chapter 12 for more discussion of this). In general, libraries should keep the minimum information needed to maintain service.

SCHOOL LIBRARIES

Libraries located in K–12 (or pre-K–12) schools typically serve the students, teachers, and staff members of the school. As you can probably imagine, this diverse patron base—including children, young adults/teens, and adults—has a wide range of reading levels and interests as well as maturity and reading comprehension. This makes intellectual freedom concerns for the school community challenging.

Differences from Public Libraries

In addition, school employees are generally understood to be legally acting in loco parentis—meaning in place of parents. This means they are legally responsible for the minors in their care and must act accordingly. This is a very different relationship than that public librarians have with the minors who are in their library. In school libraries or media centers, the librarian must act responsibly on behalf of the parents.

This difference from public libraries has a *significant* impact on intellectual freedom concerns and challenges. School librarians must simply take different factors into account and sometimes look at things from a different perspective. This does not mean, however, that intellectual freedom is an unimportant concern in school libraries. On the contrary, a school and its library may be students' only exposure to libraries, books, and literacy—in these cases, having a wide range of perspectives and views is particularly important. In fact, 81.3 percent of school librarians in a recent national survey said intellectual freedom is very important in their school (Oltmann, 2018).

Furthermore, schools are full of students learning critical thinking, becoming good citizens, and challenging preconceived notions, which means a diversity of perspectives in the school library is essential. The school library can be a place to encounter different viewpoints and consider one's own views more carefully. Students can hone the skills and approaches they learn in classrooms.

It is important, therefore, for school libraries to contain more than the "classics" or traditional perspectives. Books that feature diverse characters working through complex situations should be on the shelves (as appropriate for the grades in the school).

Having to consider age-appropriateness is another unique aspect for school librarians. For example, books and materials appropriate for high schools likely contain topics and writing levels that are inappropriate for elementary or middle school students.

This does not mean that librarians in elementary and middle schools should steer clear of complex or potentially controversial topics—just that they should select age-appropriate resources. There are numerous books, for instance, written on an elementary level that address topics such as LGBT families or the death of a loved one.

Because school employees act in loco parentis, some school librarians take parental wishes into account when determining what students can check out of a library. For example, if a family is opposed to magic, wizards, dragons, and other fantasy elements, the parents may want to restrict their children's access to these sorts of topics. Some school librarians, then, will make a note in a child's record to that effect.

Two aspects are important to mention here: first, this is only appropriate at a school library, not in a public or other type of library, where patrons have more autonomy and are responsible for themselves and their family. Second, it is important to note that such a restriction is only for the *family's* children, not for all children. In other words, a parent or guardian may restrict his or her own children's access but not the access of other children. In this way, a reasonable intellectual freedom compromise can be made.

Other Considerations

School librarians should also consider topics that may be caught in a school's internet filter. Research suggests that nearly all schools in the United States use internet filters (Jaeger & Yan, 2009), due in large part to the in loco parentis status of school employees and the fact that most students are minors.

As Chapter 10 discusses, there is wide latitude in what internet filters block and restrict. Often the internet filter is not directly under school librarians' control; there may be a technology specialist who manages internet access and usage.

Nonetheless, school librarians can act as advocates for their students, pointing out the value of allowing greater access to information. This will help students develop digital literacy as they will be better able to evaluate information online. Using less restrictive settings on the internet filter can also enable students to gain access to a wider range of information, which can benefit their growing, curious minds.

Many schools use Accelerated Reader (AR) or other similar programs to guide, track, and record students' reading levels and accomplishments. While these programs can be helpful in many ways, sometimes the ways these programs are used lead to restrictions on students' reading. For example, students may be told that they can read books only at certain levels.

To whatever extent they can, school librarians should avoid collaborating in this way. In general, librarians want students to both take pleasure in and learn from their reading, and sometimes AR and similar programs detract from the pleasurable aspect. School librarians can gently push back and do their best to encourage active, pleasurable reading that also meets educational or learning criteria as well.

Many schoolchildren attend private schools, which are often religious in funding, orientation, or tradition. The values and expectations of these private religious schools may differ from the norms of public schools, which can often affect intellectual freedom. For example, conservative Christian schools may refuse to include books with LGBT themes or non-Christian lifestyles in their libraries. This has clear ramifications for the intellectual freedom of the schools' community of learners, who may be exposed to fewer ideas and perspectives. In these situations, librarians must carefully balance their professional norms with the expectations of the school and its community; some sacrifices to intellectual freedom will likely have to be made.

ACADEMIC LIBRARIES

Academic libraries, located in universities and colleges, have somewhat different intellectual freedom concerns compared to public or school libraries. Their patron base is different—faculty, staff, and students; some institutions also have a mandate to serve their alumni and the general public, usually limited to a specific geographical area. Furthermore, their intellectual freedom concerns vary, depending on whether the library is associated with a secular or religious higher education institution.

Religious Higher Education Institutions

For those located in religious institutions, the institutional creed or belief system will generally be seen to trump professional values such as intellectual freedom; this is likely true whether the religion be Christianity, Judaism, Islam, or something else.

In other words, when there is a conflict between intellectual freedom and the religious perspective, the intellectual freedom argument will generally cede way. This is because religious higher education institutions usually put great emphasis on the importance of their beliefs.

Nonetheless, librarians in these institutions can advocate for intellectual freedom to an extent that seems reasonable in their institutions—and sometimes, it is worth pushing against the boundary of "reasonableness" to provide better access to information to the academic community.

For example, some conservative religious educational colleges have installed internet filters to block access to pornography and other information they believe would be harmful (see Chapter 10 for a detailed analysis of internet filtering).

A librarian in such an institution could argue that filters, deployed to protect adults, are restricting access to legitimate research information that could be useful to the students, faculty, and staff. Furthermore, those affiliated with the religious institution will not always be using filtered internet; in fact, most of the time in the broader world, they will encounter an unfiltered internet. To be prepared to handle the wide range of information available online, perhaps they should be able to access it while at the college, in a safer place.

Librarians should also be thoughtful about collection development and acquisition in these institutions. They may have more restrictive guidelines to follow, though here again is a place where it may make sense to question the policy. Librarians who want to collect a wide range of views, beyond the institution's orthodoxy, may be able to defend this position by pointing to the importance of questioning one's beliefs and considering alternative perspectives; many religious traditions value seeking truth and pondering different viewpoints. In order to do so, however, a library must first collect those different viewpoints.

Another concern at some religious institutions has to do with codes of conduct for students or faculty or any system that seeks to regulate and constrain behavior. Anecdotally, librarians have been asked to report circulation records, browsing habits, and other information that should be kept confidential.

For example, one librarian reported that he had collected books with several perspectives on homosexuality, contrary to the hard-line opposition of his institution's denomination. After a professor noticed these books, he demanded to know which students had checked out or shown interest in those books; presumably, the professor planned to speak to the students further. The library did not keep circulation records, so the librarian was unable to respond to the professor; however, the librarian noted that the library did not have a policy preventing this sort of query.

As we have previously discussed (see Chapter 3), privacy is an important facet of intellectual freedom. Privacy provides the freedom to explore and consider various perspectives. Librarians, even those at religious institutions, should be reluctant to violate these ideals of privacy.

Secular Higher Education Institutions

A secular higher education institution is a college or university that does *not* have a religious orientation or commitment. In practice, the line can be a bit blurry, as some universities have historical relationships with various religious denominations but no longer consider themselves bound by strict religious beliefs. The secular category also includes public universities, those that are at least partially funded by state and federal governments.

The confidentiality of library records is a concern in secular institutions as well. Faculty, for example, may want to know if students checked out certain books, asked for research assistance, or read certain articles. This often comes into play if a professor puts a book, film, or other resource on hold for students to study. All of this information should remain confidential.

As with other types of libraries, it can be a good idea to simply not collect and store this information—if something does not exist, it cannot be required to be produced. There are likely other ways to work with faculty to better help them evaluate a student's use of library resources.

As noted earlier, many secular institutions include parts of the general public (delineated by either alumni status or geographical area) as part of their patron base. Often, these patrons have limited access (e.g., requiring a physical presence in the library to access databases or smaller limits on the number of books that can be checked out). Whenever possible, librarians should advocate for more access rather than restricted access. Having different classes or groups of patrons, with different levels of access, is problematic from an intellectual freedom perspective.

Similarly, higher education institutions should try to think about licensing agreements for journals and other e-resources from an intellectual freedom perspective, if possible. These agreements often try to limit the number of users or the geographical location of users, but any limit to access is problematic, according to intellectual freedom principles. It is true that cost is usually the primary concern when negotiating these contracts, but intellectual freedom should be present in the discussions as well.

SPECIAL LIBRARIES

This is often used as a catchall category for libraries that do not fall into the public, school, or academic categories. Special libraries include hospital/medical libraries, archives, corporate or law libraries, government agency libraries, and so on (the Special Library Association's list of divisions highlights the breadth of libraries included in this category: https://www.sla.org/get-involved/divisions/; Special Library Association, n.d.).

Because this category of libraries does include such a variety, there are few broad intellectual freedom statements that can be made here. Perhaps the most important one is to consider your community—that is, your patron base—as you make decisions around intellectual freedom. For example, in a hospital library, the patrons likely include the medical staff, patients, and family members. Intellectual freedom decisions might include deciding who has what level of access to electronic databases; should all patrons have the same level of access? An intellectual freedom perspective would argue in favor of broad access, letting patients and family members access the same information as doctors and other medical staff.

In fact, special libraries do often restrict access to certain patron groups, because of their generally small budgets, resources, and capabilities. In some places, this may be appropriate: it makes sense that a corporate library might limit access to only senior officials who need the full range of information available there. Often, however, special libraries include information that would be useful to a broader patron base, if they can convince their parent institution to allow it.

Special libraries, as the previous sentence implies, are often part of a larger institution (e.g., a hospital or law firm). Because of this, the library's intellectual freedom may be constrained somewhat according to the business or legal requirements of the parent institution. Sometimes the corporate or parent institution interests are considered more important than intellectual freedom concerns; in these cases, special librarians must find reasonable ways to compromise and stand up for intellectual freedom to the extent possible. (In some ways, this is similar to the demands felt by academic librarians, who must meet their university expectations while still advocating for intellectual freedom.)

CONCLUSION

In this chapter, we have discussed how intellectual freedom impacts each type of library (public, school, academic, and special). Although the four types of libraries vary in many ways, perhaps the most pertinent difference between them is the community they serve. Each community will cause different aspects of intellectual freedom to be at the forefront. Across all of this variance, however, the importance of providing access to information, to the greatest extent possible, remains a primary concern of all libraries.

REFERENCES

American Library Association. (2013). Frequently challenged books. Document ID:82134c30-c54c-447f-be34-bfbcb7d094e5. Retrieved from http://www.ala.org/advocacy/bbooks/frequently challengedbooks

Goe, W. R., & Noonan, S. (2006). The sociology of community. In C. D. Bryant & D. L. Peck (Eds.), *21st century sociology: A reference handbook* (pp. 455–464). Thousand Oaks, CA: Sage Publications.

Jaeger, P. T., & Yan, Z. (2009). One law with two outcomes: Comparing the implementation of CIPA in public libraries and schools. *Information Technology & Libraries, 28*(1), 6–14.

Oltmann, S. M. (2018). Ethics, values, and intellectual freedom in school libraries. *School Libraries Worldwide, 24*(1), 71–86.

Special Library Association. (n.d). Divisions. Retrieved from https://www.sla.org/get-involved/divisions/

PART TWO

Intellectual Freedom in Action

SIX

How to Handle Materials Challenges

A challenge is a formal request to a library to reconsider an item in its collection. Usually challengers—that is, individuals who are challenging an item—want an item removed completely, but sometimes they ask for its relocation instead (e.g., from the children's section to the teen section). Challenges can occur in all types of libraries, though they are most common in public and school libraries (American Library Association [ALA], 2013). This chapter describes challenges in more detail, providing step-by-step guidelines for responding to concerned patrons.

First, let's start with an anecdote. One school librarian told me of an uncomfortable situation she experienced a few years ago. A parent complained that a certain book series promoted "sex without marriage" and shouldn't be in the local high school. The school had no relevant policies or guidelines about how to respond. The principal sided with the parent and essentially told the librarian to either remove the book series or lose her job. Faced with this dire situation, the librarian took the books off the shelves and hid them in her office for the rest of the semester. She did not remove them from the catalog, however. After the semester was over, she quietly put the books back into circulation without anyone noticing and has not received any more complaints.

Were her actions appropriate? Did she act as the ALA would recommend? In this chapter we describe the best way to handle materials challenges and then conclude by coming back to this anecdote and assessing it.

MATERIALS CHALLENGES

Most challenges are focused on *books* that are held in the library's collection, though other materials may be challenged, too: magazines, newspapers, CDs, DVDs, databases, internet access, and nearly every other kind of resource a library offers. Challenges may also occur with regard to library programming, displays, or other events (see Chapter 9). They often start with an angry or concerned patron; generally, that individual has read or consumed at least part of the item in question, though sometimes he or she has merely been told the item is questionable. According to the ALA, parents are the type of patron most likely to challenge materials.

This closely relates to the reasons that materials are likely to be challenged. The top three reasons that materials are challenged are due to "sexually explicit" content, "offensive language," and material that is considered "unsuited to any age group" (ALA, 2016). These reasons indicate concern that someone—a reader—could be exposed to content that is not appropriate for him or her. Most often that concern is focused on young readers and consumers of content.

Parents and guardians (and others) are sometimes reluctant to allow youth in their care to be exposed to different, sensitive, or controversial ideas, though it is important to remember, here, that everyone has a different understanding of what might be considered sensitive or controversial. In fact, calling a work "offensive" (or using any similar adjective) is entirely subjective. It depends on the people reading the work and their own unique perspectives.

Let's walk through a typical challenge scenario. It generally begins with a concerned, upset, or angry patron who wants to talk to a librarian. Sometimes he or she will take his or her own concerns to other patrons or to the media, generating uncomfortable attention for the library. Thus, it is always preferable to speak directly to the concerned individual. Many libraries have a policy that concerned patrons should speak with the library director or other degreed librarian, to ensure they're speaking with someone who is trained in an intellectual freedom background and conflict resolution. (This is a good reason to have all employees trained in intellectual freedom.)

Often, the upset patrons simply want to share their concerns or air their grievances. An important first step, then, is to listen to the patrons (LaRue, 2004). This means really paying attention to their concerns, not trying to silence or disagree with them. Let the patrons have their say. In the case of a parent concerned for a child, it might make sense to be sympathetic to the underlying motivation: "I can understand that you want to provide quality reading for your child," for example.

According to reports from librarians, often a patron just wants to be heard and doesn't want to file formal paperwork. Taking the time to listen at this stage can reduce the number of formal challenges to library materials. But, if the patron remains unsatisfied or wants to pursue the issue, then formal challenge paperwork is the next step.

FORMAL CHALLENGE PAPERWORK

When a patron is not satisfied with an informal chat about library items, the next step should be to offer official paperwork to that patron. Sometimes patrons will take, but not return, the paperwork; this is often an indication that the first step of listening was, in fact, enough to dissipate concerns.

The official paperwork is often called a "request for reconsideration." This is valuable wording, because it emphasizes the item will be *reconsidered*, not automatically removed. The paperwork formalizes the process of filing a complaint or challenge to a particular library item. (Most libraries have patrons fill out a separate form for each item that raises concerns.) Completing this paperwork has four objectives:

1.   The patron will feel that his or her concerns are taken seriously and respected by the library.

2.   The library will have documented the reason for the concern and can then analyze and address the concerns.

3.   A paperwork trail is established, which can be useful in conversations with the board of trustees, media, and others.

4.   The Office for Intellectual Freedom (OIF), a division of the ALA, can be contacted for assistance and support while the challenge is ongoing.

The ALA provides a sample policy that can be adapted to each individual library's needs at http://www.ala.org/tools/challengedmaterials/support/samplereconsideration. There are a few important notes about this sample policy.

First, the form asks if an individual is representing an organization; this is an important clarification. If there is an organization behind the individual, that may mean additional resources (e.g., time, funding, and media attention) could be spent on this challenge. While this should not change the library's approach to the challenge, it is useful information nonetheless.

Second, the policy asks whether the individual has "examined the entire resource." Similar phrasing should be used on any library's request for reconsideration form. Many items may have a word or phrase that, taken out of context, could be problematic, even offensive. However, when considered in the context of the entire content, those words and phrases are often less problematic and can be seen as a small part of the whole.

A classic example comes from *The Absolutely True Diaries of a Part-Time Indian* by Sherman Alexie. This book describes an Indian boy coming of age on a reservation, surrounded by poverty, alcohol abuse, and despair, yet finding hope through his schooling and sports. In two brief passages, the teen narrator discusses masturbation (with no graphic details). Many parents have objected to this language without seeing it in the context of a coming-of-age story of a teen boy. When the entire book is read, however, those two passages are not memorable, key excerpts. This demonstrates the importance of considering the work as a whole.

Finally, one should consider adding a brief description of the process by which the challenge will be reviewed and considered. Will an ad hoc committee be formed? Will there be an appeals process? How long will the committee take to review the material and the complaint? What form will the response take (e.g., a letter to the challenging individual)?

In addition, making key library resources available, such as the Library Bill of Rights and the local library's collection development policy, is a good idea. This provides documentation of the library's perspective on challenges and will help patrons better understand the library's point of view.

PROCESS OF CONSIDERING A CHALLENGE

One of the first steps a library should take is contacting the OIF. The OIF exists to help libraries handle challenges and prepare responses. OIF staff members have a wealth of resources and knowledge, including extensive familiarity with legal doctrine, that can aid libraries. It is reasonable and sensible to draw upon this knowledge to help your own library.

There are several ways of considering a challenge, but forming a committee to read through the challenge and analyze the material is a good idea. This takes the decision-making out of the hands of one individual and allows multiple perspectives to be represented. In addition, using a committee composed of staff members allows for a multistep appeals process: from the committee to the director to the board of trustees. Having a multistep approach helps ensure that the challengers feel their concerns are taken seriously and reviewed by multiple people. The process described here assumes a committee approach to challenges.

First, the reconsideration committee is usually *ad hoc*, meaning it is composed as needed. It should include staff from multiple levels of responsibility, if possible, including the person in charge of the collection from which the challenged material comes. Thus, the teen librarian should be on the committee when an item in the teen collection is challenged; for smaller libraries, this may mean the collection development or acquisition librarian is on most reconsideration committees, as they oversee the entire collection. This person is probably most familiar with any reviews, awards, or other relevant information pertaining to the challenged material.

All members of the committee should read, watch, or listen to the challenged item in its entirety. The timeline for this will vary depending on the size of the item (i.e., number of pages in the book) and the time constraints of the committee members. Some libraries have held a "viewing party" for all members of their committee to watch a movie in question at the same time.

After consuming the item in question, committee members should then turn to any reviews, accolades, critiques, or other media items about the challenged material. Reviews can help place the item in context; for example, a murder mystery should be considered in context of the broader genre and whether it is part of a series. In addition, reviews provide evidence for how experts view the work and can provide information about the appropriate age for the material (this is especially important for children's and teen works). Awards, reviews, and critiques provide further context about how the work was critically received and viewed by experts. A book that has won awards for its portrayal of teen angst, for example, may be particularly relevant and appropriate for teen readers; the awards in this case provide intellectual weight to keeping the item and counterbalancing the challenge.

Throughout the reconsideration process, committee members need to be cognizant of their library's collection development policy (see Chapter 7) and any other relevant policies (e.g., policies about age appropriateness, intellectual freedom, and parental supervision). Committee members may want to reread these policies or, at the very least, keep them nearby so that they can be referred to as needed.

It is also helpful to review relevant policies and documents from the ALA, including the Library Bill of Rights, the Intellectual Freedom and

Censorship Q&A, the Freedom to Read Statement, and the Core Values. These will help frame the library's immediate concerns—focused on a single work—in the broader context of library ethics and values. It is essential that this broader view not be lost.

Once the item in question has been read or viewed, along with reviews, awards, and relevant policies, committee members should carefully consider the challenge at hand. It should not be simply dismissed; a patron has taken the time to communicate something important to them, and it should be treated as such. This means reading the challenge with respect and compassion. Consider it carefully.

Here are some questions to think through: Does the patron raise valid concerns? Are the concerns reflected or addressed in reviews or other external information? Do these concerns trump any positive effects of the item? Who is the audience for the item (according to reviews or the publisher)? Is this an appropriate audience for the item? Was the item catalogued properly and placed in the appropriate location for this audience (i.e., a book for teens should be cataloged in the teen section)? Are the concerns mitigated by other aspects of the book (e.g., the overall theme or message)? Are the concerns focused on a small portion of the item or the overall/entire item? These questions should be discussed as a committee, with frequent referral to external reviews, library policies, and ALA statements. Throughout this process, the item in question should be kept on the shelves and maintained in the collection; while some individuals may want to remove the challenged item, this can create a presumption in favor of permanent removal.

DECIDING WHAT TO DO

Once a challenged item has been carefully considered, there are four basic outcomes that can occur. First, the challenged item could be removed from general circulation. Second, the item could be retained in the collection. Third, the item may be moved within the collection. Finally, there are a few less common responses that are considered "other options." Let's review each of these in detail.

Common Options

First, challenged items are sometimes removed from library collections. The general sentiment is that this happens rarely. Certainly, in the data that the ALA has collected, few libraries report that they have removed items (although it is worth noting that the ALA acknowledges its data are incomplete). There is a strong normative opposition to this option: it is counter to librarian ethics and core values and is in contrast to the strong stances of the Library Bill of Rights and the Freedom to Read Statement. This is the removal of some information from circulation, preventing others from accessing it. The removal of challenged items should be done extremely rarely. This is, essentially, *censorship* of the item in question.

Most of the time, challenged items are retained in the collection. After consideration, committee members determine that the item fits the collection development policy and is appropriate to keep in the collection. If this is the decision, the item should be kept in the collection with little fanfare, though a letter of explanation should be written to the challenger (see later this chapter).

A third option, undertaken especially frequently with children's and teen resources, is to relocate the material. Imagine a book is cataloged as juvenile fiction, but upon a challenge and a review, the committee determines the item should really be in the young adult section. Generally, items get shifted "upward" in age—from children's to juvenile, from juvenile to teen, or from teen to adult. This is usually done because people determine the content and/or themes are too mature for the first audience and are more appropriate for an older audience.

Care must be taken, however, that this is actually true. Sometimes, in order to appease challengers, committees decide to move an item that really does not need to be moved. Perhaps the juvenile fiction book really is written for a juvenile audience, with juvenile vocabulary and an age-appropriate handling of difficult or complex themes. In this case, it would be inappropriate to relocate the book simply to satisfy the challenger. Rather, the item should be retained in the juvenile section and its placement carefully explained and defended.

Less Common Options

Finally, there are a few options that are exercised less often but still need to be considered. One of these options is to take a controversial item and place it "behind the desk," in the librarian's office, or in a special section with restricted access. These materials are then only accessed with special permission or upon verbal request by a patron. This generally results in de facto censorship, meaning no one knows about or requests the item, so it functions the same as censorship.

There was a rural library, not too long ago, that dared to buy and catalog *The Joy of Gay Sex* by Charles Silverstein and Edmund White. After a challenge, the library moved the book to a book truck kept in the basement. The staff argued that the book was still in the catalog and patrons could still request it. But the publicness of asking for this book at the library desk meant it did not circulate. Its location was a form of subtle censorship. Thus, this option (restricted access) should be viewed with suspicion, as its effect is often a lack of access.

Another option exercised by some libraries is to keep the book on a shelf but take it out of the catalog, making it difficult to find. This is another form of de facto censorship, again limiting patrons' access to it. Other options include marking out offensive words, removing pages with offensive passages, trying to cut or splice problematic words or images from music and films, and various other forms of redaction.

These are not merely hypothetical options. The 2007 Newberry Award winner, *The Higher Power of Lucky* (by Susan Patron), set off a controversy because the word "scrotum" was on the very first page. It was in the context of a story about a dog being bit by a rattlesnake. But some librarians, concerned about this word, argued they would either not buy the book or would try to redact the word with black marker (Bosman, 2007). In the end, very few libraries reported any challenges to the book and the furor died down.

In another case, a library in Iowa reorganized its entire collection to segregate the LGBT items in it. After facing several challenges to books with LGBT themes and mounting negative publicity, the Orange City Public Library decided to group books by category and subject rather than the author name (Associated Press, 2018).

All of these various approaches should be seen as forms of censorship and attempts to appease challengers. While some individuals may be satisfied with these attempts, they violate the spirit and sense of library ethics and core values.

Writing a Letter to the Challenger

Regardless of which action is chosen, the committee should draft a letter to the challenger. This letter should:

1. note that the committee members carefully considered the challenge;

2. explain members read or viewed the item in question;

3. refer to external reviews and other information as appropriate;

4. refer to the library's collection development policy; and

5. inform the patron what action has been taken.

In general, the letter should be written as a neutral explanation of the library's thoughts and decision, not in a defensive, condescending, or challenging tone. It is a good idea to describe the appeals process, if it exists, and to thank the patrons for their concern and willingness to go through the process. Again, this is a patron who cares enough about the library and its collection to fill out paperwork and express concern, so it seems reasonable to be respectful in return. The letter should come from the senior member of the committee on behalf of the library; the entire process and the letter should then be summarized and shared with the director and board of trustees, if applicable.

When writing the letter, many library directors will quote from the First Amendment or relevant ALA policies, such as the Library Bill of Rights, the Freedom to Read Statement, or the Core Values. The goal here is to convey the importance of access to information from the library's perspective. One public library director shared his approach, stating that he generally includes the following information:

> The library seeks to provide materials that represent a variety of viewpoints, ideas, and concepts. The First Amendment to our Constitution affords the library its role as a provider of diverse materials to the community it serves, endows the artist with the freedom to express him/herself as seen fit, as well as bestowing the individual right of citizens to freely express their beliefs on the validity of those same items. When we discuss these issues, whether supporting or objecting to a work, we are practicing our right to freedom of speech guaranteed by our Constitution.

BOARD OF TRUSTEES' ROLE

Many public libraries, some academic libraries, and some other types of libraries have boards of trustees or similar oversight bodies. This brief section is written for those institutions. In general, reserve the board of trustees to serve as a step in an appeals process (see previous discussion).

However, this presupposes that your board of trustees has been trained in intellectual freedom, is well-versed with the collection development policy, and supports the core values and principles of librarianship. (If you are not sure whether this is the case for your board, you should start training them now, before such training needs to be acted upon!)

In situations where an item has been challenged, boards of trustees can serve two important functions. First, they can act as public ambassadors for your institution. These individuals can be promoting the library and its values out in the community, building support for pro-intellectual freedom stances. This can be essential for swaying public opinion and, regardless of whether you face a challenge, can build goodwill for the library.

Second, oversight boards can serve as a stop on the appeals process. Let's say a committee reviewed an item, determined it should be kept in the library collection, and sent a letter to that effect to the challenger. If the challenger is unsatisfied with this response, he or she may want to challenge it further. He or she may take the appeal to the board of trustees. Once this is done, the board should follow a similar procedure to the reconsideration committee (see earlier). This will help assure the challenger that his or her concerns are taken seriously.

DEALING WITH THE MEDIA AND THE PUBLIC

In the previous section, we briefly discussed how the board of trustees can aid with public perception. The public perception of a challenge situation can be quite important. There are a few important considerations for libraries of all types; "public" here refers not only to the general population served by a public library but also to a library's *potential* patron base and supporters, however broad or general that may be. Both academic and school libraries, along with public libraries, have encountered publicity from challenges. The public can also extend far beyond one's local community, if a national organization gets involved (either supporting or opposing the challenge) or if the issue starts trending on social media.

One important consideration is the role of the media (which includes, these days, social media). Some challengers (or the organizations of which they are a part) may contact the media, attempting to stir up controversy and negative publicity for the library. Often, when the challenge is to a children's or teen item, it is portrayed as a danger to innocent youth. This is a narrative that can be quite dangerous to the library, as it has the potential to negatively sway the public. Thus, libraries must act quickly and decisively to counter such a narrative.

Library Spokesperson

The first step is to simply designate a library spokesperson (if there is not already one); usually this is the library director or another senior administrative person who is well-versed in library policy and library ethics. Try to funnel all media communication through this person, to keep the library messaging consistent and adherent to library values. The last thing a library would want in this situation is for library staff members to rush to judgment and support a challenge. Instead, the challenge should be dealt with as it would be without the media attention: through a considerate, thoughtful process that carefully reviews the work, external reviews, library policies, and ALA statements.

In communicating with the media, the library spokesperson should strike a careful balance between supporting patrons' rights to challenge material and the library's pro-intellectual freedom stance. If the challenge concerns children's or teen materials, the library must not appear to condone inappropriate content (while, at the same time, not automatically rejecting a challenged item as inappropriate). This all ties back to giving the challengers (and the public, once the public is aware of the challenge) assurance that their concerns will be taken seriously and respected. A nuanced and thoughtful statement at this stage can dissipate negative publicity.

It is important to state library values and ethics in such a way that others can understand and support them as well. To do so, we must leave our jargon behind. Most of the general public has never heard the term "intellectual freedom" and may not intuitively support it. A general argument is "If someone wanted books supporting your point of view removed, you wouldn't like that, and that is why we have books supporting all points of view. No one's perspective gets removed from the library." This can often be expanded upon or made more meaningful with personal examples.

It can also be helpful to explain that parents can choose, or help their children choose, what is read in their homes, but they can't choose what is read in other homes. Parents have the right (and the responsibility) to guide their own children. However, this does not mean some parents can decide what is appropriate for *all* children. Finally, emphasizing the library's fair, reasonable reconsideration process is important as well.

Board of Trustees' Meetings

If the challenge is to be discussed at a board of trustees' meeting (or if the challenge gets appealed to the board of trustees), you should investigate whether this meeting is required by law to be open to the public. For many public libraries, as well as public schools and state-funded universities, such meetings fall under "Open Records" laws and must be accessible to the public. This means that the general public—especially concerned citizens—might attend and want to comment on the situation at hand. If the meeting is required to be open, do not try to conduct the meeting in secret; this will only lead to more negative publicity and disapproval from the public.

Instead, fashion fair and reasonable guidelines, such as allowing anyone to speak on the topic of the challenge for two minutes. This will allow for an airing of diverse viewpoints and will allow the concerned individuals to have their say in a public forum. Official library policy should still be followed regarding the challenge, regardless of what the public sentiment seems to be, though care must be taken to explain why an item is retained, removed, or relocated.

As the previous sentence implies, there may be tension between public sentiment ("remove this evil book") and the library's decision regarding the challenge. At this point, it is probably reasonable to acknowledge such tension while explaining the library decision. If the decision is to retain the challenged item, explain the reasoning; here, we can see the importance of following a consistent and well-thought-out process. Having (and following) such a process will show the impartiality of the library and how its core values are applied.

ROLE OF TRAINING

Throughout this chapter, it should have become clear that the library director needs to have a strong foundation in intellectual freedom in order to meet challenges appropriately. Similarly, it is important to provide training to the board of trustees (if your institution has one) so that they can provide public support to the library.

Beyond that, though, all members of the library should be trained in intellectual freedom matters, particularly in how to handle challenges. The institution should have a clearly delineated policy that everyone follows, whenever a patron wants to challenge an item. This can demonstrate impartiality to the challenger. It can also protect staff from an upset patron, because the first step in such a policy is usually to get a senior-level staff member (often, the director) to talk directly to the concerned patron.

Encountering an upset patron, as many librarians know, is not a fun experience. It is a good idea to walk staff through the expectations and perhaps role-play what they should do if someone wants to challenge materials. This training should be done regularly so that it stays fresh in staff members' minds.

Finally, the request for reconsideration form should be kept at all service points or desks. Make sure the staff know where it is and when to offer it to patrons. This should be seen as just another way to provide service.

CONCLUSION

This chapter has discussed the appropriate ways to handle challenges to library materials, applicable in all types of libraries. The primary steps include listening to the concerned patron, giving them a form to complete, reviewing the challenged item, making a determination about what the library will do, and sending a response letter to the challenger.

Perhaps the most common response is to keep the challenged item— and this is in line with intellectual freedom principles. Removing an item or relocating it generally results in censorship: fewer people (or no one) can access it.

With these principles in mind, let's reconsider the anecdote from the beginning of the chapter. The school librarian in that case was faced with a stark choice: lose her job or remove the books in question. Without any policies or guidelines to support her taking a stand, the decision to (temporarily) remove the books seems understandable.

Hopefully, her next steps were to write a collection development policy and a reconsideration policy. Having these formal documents would help her better defend intellectual freedom to her principal and to the concerned parent. They could use the reconsideration policy to determine if the books were truly inappropriate or not.

REFERENCES

American Library Association. (2013). Infographics. Retrieved from http://www.ala.org/advocacy/bbooks/frequentlychallengedbooks/ statistics. Document ID: c0c18554-4768-4e74-b600-aaba4d4d80dd.

American Library Association. (2016). Banned books FAQ. Retrieved from http://www.ala.org/advocacy/bbooks/banned-books-qa. Document ID: 7b34cc98-f94b-466b-80c5-392c3dd04e55.

Associated Press. (2018). Orange City Library shifts policy after outcry over LGBT materials. KCRG.com. Retrieved from https://www.kcrg.com/content/news/Orange-City-library-shifts-policy-after-outcry-over-LGBT-materials-477532033.html

Bosman, J. (2007). With one word, children's book sets off uproar. *New York Times*. Retrieved from https://www.nytimes.com/2007/02/18/books/18newb.html

LaRue, J. (2004). Buddha at the gate, running: Why people challenge library materials. *American Libraries, 35*(11), 42–44.

SEVEN

Collection Development and Weeding

Collection development is an essential part of building and maintaining a library's collection (of books, audiovisual materials, or any other materials). Although some people may not realize it, strong intellectual freedom concerns arise with collection development.

Because collection development is, fundamentally, about the library's collection, it is a central locus for the application of intellectual freedom principles. In this chapter, we review the importance of having a strong collection development policy and a balanced collection, and we discuss the intellectual freedom implications of evaluating and weeding a collection.

In a recent research project on collection development and intellectual freedom, I asked midwestern librarians about their collection development practices. One librarian responded, "We have migrated from a completely balanced collection as our budget is small and our patrons are very specific about their tastes" (Oltmann, 2019).

This is a good starting point for our discussion about collection development in light of intellectual freedom principles. Is that statement problematic? If so, in what ways? What intellectual freedom concerns might we have regarding this library's collection? How can those concerns be mitigated?

COLLECTION DEVELOPMENT POLICY

It is very important to have a written collection development policy for your library. It will serve multiple functions. First, a collection development policy helps guide the selection and acquisition of materials for the library. When you aren't sure whether a book is a good selection for your library, the collection development policy should provide concrete guidance to making that decision. The policy provides formal structure to such decisions. Second, a collection development policy can be seen as a statement of what is important to your library and how you ensure it gets collected for your library. Third, a collection development policy can provide protection and assistance if an item in the collection is ever challenged. We focus on the third function in this chapter.

If you do not currently have a collection development policy, you can start developing one by contacting your state library organization for assistance. You can also contact libraries in your area and ask if they would be willing to share their policies with you; then you can use these policies as a guide to forming your own. There are also numerous texts that describe and explain key aspects of a collection development policy.

Key Components of a Collection Development Policy

All collection development policies should contain five components: a description of the library and its patrons, a list of criteria by which materials are selected, a statement about intellectual freedom, referral to a reconsideration policy (see Chapter 6), and referral to key statements from the American Library Association (ALA).

The description of the library and its patrons sets the scene for rest of the policy. This should describe the type of library (public, academic, school, medical, etc.) and its mission or purpose. The mission may vary depending upon the type of library, and this should guide selection decisions, so it is good to be clear and specific here.

Avoid describing the population that is served with overly specific demographic detail for two reasons. First, demographics can change quickly and that would cause you to have to change the policy frequently. Second, by focusing on some demographic numbers, you may be excluding segments of the population. For example, if your patron base is 83 percent white, this does not mean that you can overlook the 17 percent of the population that consists of people of color. In fact, your collection development policy should specifically *include* small segments of the population and those who might traditionally be overlooked.

Many books on collection development offer lists of suggested criteria for selecting materials. Johnson (2018) offers the following list:

- Content or subject
- Language
- Currency
- Veracity (truthfulness, accuracy)
- Writing style (well written, easy to read, aesthetic aspects)
- Completeness and scope of treatment
- Reputation, credential, or authoritativeness of author, publisher, editor, reviewers
- Instructional design, if intended to meet certain instructional objectives
- Geographic coverage
- Quality of scholarship
- Frequency of the title's reference in bibliographies or citations
- Reading or user level to which the content is directed
- Frequency of updates or revisions
- Access points (indexes, level of detail in the table of contents)
- Ease of use
- External resources that index the publication
- Physical quality (illustrations, paper and binding, format, typography, durability, visual and audio characteristics)
- Uniqueness of content, capabilities, or features
- Availability of equipment required for hearing or viewing audiovisual material
- Cost in relation to quality of item and its projected use (p. 126)

Some of these components will be more or less important to different libraries or different types of collections. For example, an academic library looking to expand its collection of audiobooks will certainly want to weigh the types of equipment needed to use various books. A children's librarian will likely put more emphasis on illustrations and binding durability than, say, an adult collection development librarian. Whichever factors are most important and relevant for your particular library should be *clearly articulated* in the collection development policy.

It is important for the collection development policy to include statements about the significance of intellectual freedom. This establishes that intellectual freedom is a key consideration when building and evaluating the collection. If items are challenged, the library staff can use the collection development policy as evidence that intellectual freedom is important to the library.

The collection development policy can also include reference to the reconsideration policy, establishing a relationship between the two. Essentially, when an item is challenged (asked to be reconsidered), library staff should turn to the collection development policy to see if the item meets the collection objectives contained there (see Chapter 6 for more about reconsideration).

Finally, inclusion of key documents from the ALA serves a similar purpose: this establishes the importance of the relationship between the local library and the ALA, as well as the structure for evaluating reconsideration challenges in light of documents such as the Freedom to Read Statement and Library Bill of Rights. These documents serve as reminders of the purpose of the library and the purpose of its collection (of any type of items). These are important to keep in mind when one is forming and evaluating the collection.

In other words, the collection cannot be based on the whims or preferences of a single individual (or a small group of librarians) but must be designed for the entire community that is being served. The Freedom to Read Statement and the Library Bill of Rights will help keep these priorities foremost.

Any collection development policy should be reviewed by an attorney and by the board of trustees. The attorney should ensure that the policy does not contain anything illegal; this is often a formality with collection development policies, but it is a good practice to develop.

The board of trustees should be quite familiar with library policies, as the trustees serve as a bridge between the community and the library. If the board is familiar with the policies, they can represent and explain the policies to community members who have questions or concerns. In addition, a collection development policy that includes pro-intellectual freedom statements and documents from the ALA will help remind the board about the importance and centrality of intellectual freedom.

COLLECTING CONTROVERSIAL ITEMS

Inevitably, your library will have to deal with collecting potentially controversial items at some point. This is true for all types of libraries (but may be particularly relevant for public and school libraries, which often face more challenges). There are basically three ways to approach this truism: thoughtfully acquire controversial items, purposefully avoid controversial items whenever possible, or take a more haphazard approach, neither deliberate collecting nor avoiding. The haphazard approach should be avoided because it leaves you unprepared for potential challenges and means you are not approaching collection development in a thoughtful, engaged manner.

Trying to avoid controversial items is a losing proposition: you cannot predict with certainty what will be controversial, and trying to avoid all controversy will lead to a weakened, deficient collection. As we have discussed elsewhere in the book, controversy is subjective.

For example, some people may think that fiction, nonfiction, or films depicting police brutality are harmful to societal well-being; they may think these works do not belong in a library. In contrast, other people may believe that these items are necessary in the library and serve the valuable purpose of counterbalancing a mostly benign, positive portrayal of law enforcement.

Either the inclusion or exclusion of these items—or, for different groups, *both* the inclusion and exclusion—could be controversial positions, depending on the composition of your community and which particular patrons are engaged with the library.

A Thoughtful Approach

The third approach—having a deliberate, well-reasoned approach to collection development—will reduce stress, anxiety, and possible negative publicity; this will also create a well-rounded, diverse, and appealing collection. The first principle here is to ensure that an item is not rejected immediately because it is (or could be) controversial to some in your community.

This was a concern in 2013 with the publication of *Two Boys Kissing*, a teen book by David Levithan. The book focuses on two boys who want to break the world record for the longest kiss and features an image of two boys kissing on its cover. Many librarians hesitated to acquire this item because of its title and cover art, which were unapologetic in their portrayal of a gay relationship. (The book made the Top Ten Most Challenged Books Lists in 2015 and 2016; ALA, 2013.)

Instead of focusing on whether the item will be perceived as controversial, the item should be considered on its *merits* and in light of the collection development policy. For example, if the policy states a preference for well-reviewed items, has this particular item received strong reviews? That consideration should carry more weight than any potential controversy.

Asheim (1953) wrote an important essay considering selection versus censorship and explaining the differences between the two principles. He wrote,

> For to the selector, the important thing is to find reasons to keep the book. Given such a guiding principle, the selector looks for values, for strengths, for virtues which will over shadow [*sic*] minor objections. For the censor, on the other hand, the important thing is to find reasons to reject the book; his guiding principle leads him to seek out the objectionable features, the weaknesses, the possibilities for misinterpretation. . . . The selector says, if there is anything good in this book let us try to keep it; the censor says, if there is anything bad in this book, let us reject it.

Asheim's argument was that librarians act as *selectors*, not as censors, for their community. We should adopt a similar mind-set when deciding whether to purchase a new, potentially controversial item for the collection.

Are there positive attributes to the item? Does it have values, strengths, or virtues? Does this item meet the standards of the collection development policy? (Here, we can see one very important reason to have a written formalized policy.) Does the book speak to a particular part of your community—especially one that may be marginalized or underrepresented in the collection? If the answers to these questions are yes, then the item should be acquired, regardless of whether it may stir controversy.

Many items that librarians suspect could be controversial turn out to be well accepted and regarded by the community—or at least well read. For example, many librarians were concerned about *50 Shades of Grey* (by E. L. James) and its reception in their communities. While it was frequently challenged (ALA, 2013), it was also well read. There are many anecdotal reports of large "hold" lists for the book and of conservative but curious readers. In many communities, the book was not challenged at all. A fear of *possible* controversy is not a good reason to decline purchasing an item.

At the same time, some items stir unanticipated controversy. It is impossible to accurately predict which materials will be poorly received and challenged by your community, so concern about a possible challenge is not a good foundation for making collection development decisions.

BALANCED COLLECTIONS

One important consideration in building and maintaining a library collection is the issue of *balance*. In general, most libraries should aim for having multiple perspectives and viewpoints available in the collection. Recall that intellectual freedom "provides for free access to all expressions of ideas through which *any and all* sides of a question, cause or movement may be explored" (ALA, 2007, para. 1, emphasis added).

Thus, having a balanced collection is a way of fulfilling the principle of intellectual freedom. Because intellectual freedom is a core value of librarianship, having a balanced collection is very important.

Balance does not necessarily mean that there are an exactly equal number of books with opposing viewpoints—for example, your library does not necessarily need four books by Republicans and four books by Democrats to be balanced. Looking only at numbers is a simplistic understanding of balance and doesn't do justice to the collection or to your patrons.

In the case of political books, for example, you might consider whether your collection includes books with socialist, communist, and libertarian perspectives in addition to the two dominant parties. Are minority viewpoints represented in the collection? Instead of focusing on numbers, think about representing the breadth of views on a particular topic. It may be refreshing and enlightening to include perspectives that your patrons do not encounter elsewhere.

Some specialized libraries or highly focused collections may not need to have the same degree of balance that most other libraries ought to strive for; for example, a medical library located in a hospital probably does not need to include information about treatment alternatives unsupported by scientific evidence—and this should be explained and defended in the collection development policy.

Library Bill of Rights

There are some principles from the Library Bill of Rights that are relevant here. The first principle says, in part, "Materials should not be excluded because of the origin, background, or views of those contributing to their creation" (ALA, 2006, para. 1). The second principle adds, "Materials should not be proscribed or removed because of partisan or doctrinal disapproval" (para. 2). This means that the background or views of the creator (author, producer, etc.) are irrelevant to whether we collect the item; likewise, the partisan beliefs of the creators should not be taken into account.

Thus, a librarian may strongly disagree with politicians of a certain political party, but their background should be irrelevant when deciding whether to acquire their books. Instead, we should be considering whether their books will add to the balance of the collection and whether the books meet the guidelines of the collection development policy.

For example, many librarians were unsure whether to acquire a book written by Milo Yiannopoulos (*Dangerous*) in 2017. He was well known for disseminating hate speech; in fact, major publishers declined to be associated with him by publishing his book. But he was also a famous figure with a message that many wanted to hear: Should libraries thus carry his book?

In this case, the background of Yiannopoulos and his partisan messages should *not* factor into the decision. Libraries instead turned to their collection development policies, and many found that *Dangerous* did not meet their collection development standards (e.g., it was poorly reviewed and poorly written), and as a result, they did not purchase the book.

There are two ways to arrive at the same conclusion: don't buy the book. One route starts by focusing on Yiannopoulos's hate speech, his message, and his politics. The other route starts by evaluating the book on its merits. Although both may arrive at the same destination, there is an important difference between these two paths: the second path does not *prejudge* the book or its content. It thoughtfully considers whether this is appropriate and relevant for the library and its patrons. This is an intellectual freedom foundation for collection development.

Balance and Diversity

In general, all libraries should aim to represent a wide range of views. Johnson (2018) explains,

Balanced coverage means selecting materials that represent all viewpoints on important and controversial issues. More recently, librarians have sought to select materials that depict diversity in all areas—race, ethnicity, gender, sexual orientation, socioeconomic status, age, physical abilities, religious beliefs, and political beliefs— and to build collections that reflect the multiplicity of contemporary society. (pp. 23–24)

As Johnson implies, a balanced collection including a wide range of views practically necessitates having diverse authors and publishers. This may mean going beyond the most common sources of information for collection development librarians. For example, there are several small presses that specialize in LGBT fiction, which is often overlooked by the largest publishing houses. If you relied solely on lists and reviews from the largest publishers, many LGBT items would not be selected and the collection would be far less balanced.

Having a balanced collection is one way to serve your community, regardless of how diverse (or not) the community may be. Even if the community is mostly of one political mind, for instance, it is worthwhile to include some opposing or alternative viewpoints in the collection. Community members may want to educate themselves on opponents or consider different perspectives. Seeing there is a range of views on a particular issue may help others form their own opinions.

Of course, "diversity" is a very broad term and is used in many different ways. Here, we mean diversity in terms of authors/creators, diversity of main and secondary characters, diversity of publishers/producers, and points of view. Diversity can encompass differences in race and ethnicity, gender, sexuality, able-bodiedness, religion, politics, socioeconomic status, veteran status, and so on.

For example, does your collection contain items by authors of different races? Items that feature characters from different socioeconomic backgrounds? Items from mainstream and independent publishers? Items that take on different religious viewpoints? These are just a few examples and may or may not be relevant for your particular library—again, you should turn to the collection development policy and purpose of the library, as well as consider your patrons.

Data collected by the Office of Intellectual Freedom (OIF) show that books with diverse main characters are disproportionately challenged. As the OIF describes, this includes "non-white main and/or secondary characters; LGBT main and/or secondary characters; disabled main and/or secondary characters; issues about race or racism; LGBT issues; issues about religion, which encompass in this situation the Holocaust and terrorism;

issues about disability and/or mental illness; non-Western settings, in which the West is North America and Europe" (ALA, 2016, para. 4). In addition, diverse books are often collected less frequently than books with white, heterosexual characters. In this sense, books with diverse characters face double discrimination.

Intellectual freedom, by advocating for all points of view, serves as an important defense for collecting and maintaining diverse books (Oltmann, 2017). Oltmann argues,

> As a principle, intellectual freedom encourages (perhaps even requires) the presence of diverse perspectives and voices. Intellectual freedom, with its insistence that all voices be available, implies that diverse books should be part of library resources. If one does not have certain diverse viewpoints present, is intellectual freedom really being upheld? (p. 415)

EVALUATING AND WEEDING A COLLECTION

A strong collection development policy, as described earlier, can help guide and shape the development of a library's collection. However, most libraries are not starting from scratch; they already have extensive collections that they may need to evaluate, reconsider, and expand. Even if a library was starting from zero items, it would want to evaluate the collection as it grew.

Evaluation is generally used as a starting point to weeding a collection—that is, removing items from the collection. There are many ways to evaluate a collection, and this section cannot address them all. Considerations often include recency of collection (the average year of publication of items), circulation frequency, wear and tear of items, relevancy, and accuracy. Several models to guide evaluation (and eventual deselection) have been developed. Evaluating a collection and subsequent weeding are essential to maintaining a healthy, vibrant collection and should be undertaken regularly.

Intellectual Freedom Concerns When Weeding a Collection

Here, our focus is on the intellectual freedom considerations when evaluating a collection; there are three concerns that should be addressed.

First, there is often a temptation to be critical of items that are controversial or have been challenged previously. Perhaps there is a book that has generated controversy within one's community. For example, *The Kite Runner*, by Khaled Hosseini, has been on the Top Ten Most Challenged Books Lists repeatedly (ALA, 2013) for offensive language and depiction of sexual violence.

It might seem simple to negatively evaluate this item, based on wear, accuracy, popularity within the community, and so on, and then decide to deselect the book. Evaluation of the collection provides a convenient point at which one could remove controversial (or potentially controversial) items.

However, items should *not* be removed because they are, or could be, controversial. As we have discussed previously, conceptions of "controversial" are highly subjective, varying from person to person. In addition, controversy in and of itself is never a sufficient reason to remove something; none of the formal models of collection evaluation suggest removing items simply because they are controversial. Rather, controversial items should be evaluated in the same way that all other items are.

Second, special care needs to be taken when evaluating items for accuracy. This applies most clearly to medical or technological information, which tends to change rapidly. The concept of "accuracy" is more difficult to apply to politics, religion/spirituality, and socioeconomic issues, on which perspectives vary widely. A good example here is climate change. The science of climate change is well known and well settled, but there are numerous opinions that are contradictory—and some anticlimate change perspectives are quite popular.

Which items get included in a library? At this point, we should turn to the collection development policy and the purpose of the library. These will guide our selection decisions around controversial items, including more or less accurate positions.

Third, when evaluating a collection, the diversity of items needs to be considered. If diverse books are not circulating well in the library and are slated to be weeded, the library should replace those books and take special efforts to encourage the new books' circulation—such as featuring these books in displays and programming. The overall diversity of the collection is one way to measure the health of the collection; if weeding reduces the diversity, then newly acquired materials should refresh and expand the diversity of the collection.

CONCLUSION

In this chapter, we have explored collection development from an intellectual freedom perspective. We have discussed the importance of a solid collection development policy, which includes reference to fundamental ALA documents like the Freedom to Read Statement and the Library Bill of Rights. When collecting items, it is important to evaluate them on their merits, without regard to whether they may generate controversy with your patrons. It is important to approach potentially controversial items thoughtfully.

Collections should be balanced—that does not mean numerically balanced, which is likely not possible, but balanced in terms of coverage and breadth. Consider having a multiplicity of views represented to serve your patrons. In addition, collections should be diverse; a well-balanced collection will represent a diversity of perspectives. Balance and diversity can be seen as complementary goals when building a collection.

Finally, when weeding a collection, be sure to once again consider items in a thoughtful manner. Though it may be tempting to deselect items that have been controversial, that is not a sufficient or appropriate reason to remove items from the collection.

Now that we've viewed collection development from an intellectual freedom perspective, let's return to the anecdote at the beginning of the chapter, in which the librarian reported no longer having a balanced collection because their patrons had specific tastes. Now, we can see that this stance is problematic. Letting the most vociferous patrons dictate the balance present in the collection means the librarian is abdicating their professional duties. A collection that is out of balance is probably not serving the community well. It may lack diversity and items that would be of interest to their patrons, if they were present.

REFERENCES

American Library Association. (2006). Library bill of rights. Retrieved from http://www.ala.org/advocacy/intfreedom/librarybill. Document ID: 669fd6a3-8939-3e54–7577-996a0a3f8952.

American Library Association. (2007). Intellectual freedom and censorship Q&A. Retrieved from http://www.ala.org/advocacy/intfreedom/censorship/faq. Document ID: e8ae9ed7-a469-f0d4-adf0-f2770d2ca8e8.

American Library Association. (2013). Top ten most challenged books lists. Retrieved from http://www.ala.org/advocacy/bbooks/frequently challengedbooks/top10#2013. Document ID: 8417fa9e-ceff-4512-aca9-9fbc81b8bd81.

American Library Association. (2016). Defining diversity. Retrieved from http://www.ala.org/advocacy/bbooks/diversity. Document ID: 2812e03d-d3ff-4d46-a34e-151dff980bee.

Asheim, L. (1953). Not censorship but selection. *Wilson Library Bulletin, 28*, 63–67.

Johnson, P. (2018). *Fundamentals of collection development and management* (4th ed.). Chicago, IL: American Library Association.

Oltmann, S.M. (2017). Creating space at the table: Intellectual freedom can bolster diverse voices. *Library Quarterly, 87*(4), 410–418.

Oltmann, S.M. (2019). Important factors in midwestern public librarians' views on intellectual freedom and collection development (Part II). *Library Quarterly, 89*(2), 156–172.

EIGHT

Addressing the #MeToo Movement in Literature

In this chapter, we discuss the #MeToo movement in the context of libraries and intellectual freedom. The #MeToo movement, which has been gaining momentum since 2016, identifies people (usually men) who are accused of sexual misconduct (including harassment, assault, and other negative, often poorly defined behavior).

Typically, these accused people have not been charged or found guilty of crimes in a court of law. Usually there are multiple accusers who come forward, reinforcing one another's story. For example, multiple women may accuse a certain man of sexually harassing them, usually in the same fashion over a period of time.

Although not in literature, comedian Louis C.K. is a noteworthy example of a man who was accused by multiple women of sexual misconduct (Framke, 2017; Ryzik, Buckley, & Kantor, 2017). He admitted his misconduct and faded rather quickly from the public (although he has tried to mount a comeback; see Ryzik, 2018). Most people accused of sexual

This chapter is revised and updated from Shannon M. Oltmann, "How Should Libraries Respond to #MeToo? Consulting Our Values and Collection Policies in the Face of the Movement," *American Libraries* (June 1, 2018), https://americanlibrariesmagazine.org/2018/06/01/how-should-libraries-respond-to-metoo/.

misconduct do *not* admit to this behavior but instead try to deflect and defend themselves.

The complexities of addressing #MeToo in the library world can be illustrated by considering the Little Bill series of children's books written by Bill Cosby in the 1990s. (Cosby was convicted of sexual assault in 2018; see Benshoff & Allyn, 2018.) A midsized public library in the southwestern United States grappled with this issue recently, after patrons brought several Little Bill books to the circulation desk and asked if they could be removed. A quick search in the catalog revealed some additional books by Bill Cosby, such as a nonfiction title *Love and Marriage* (1990). The librarians wondered if these were appropriate to keep in the collection, especially after his conviction.

How can and should librarians respond when authors and other creators are accused of sexual misconduct? How can intellectual freedom principles inform our decision-making in this regard?

THE CONTEXT OF THE #METOO MOVEMENT

The MeToo movement began in 2007 with Tarana Burke, an activist who formed a nonprofit organization to help victims of sexual assault and harassment (Garcia, 2017). It gained steam in 2017 when the hashtag #MeToo soared in popularity across Twitter, the social media platform where many women shared their stories and reassured one another that they were not alone—in effect, saying, "This happened to me too." Waves of #MeToo activism have swept multiple industries and disciplines, and literature is no different.

Numerous authors, illustrators, and others associated with publishing have been implicated in the #MeToo movement. Many of the accused are in children and young adult literature, but they span the entire industry; in addition, many of the accused are best-selling, widely popular authors. This chapter will not provide a list of the accused or the salacious details, which are available online for those who want to know more (see Cohen & Hus, 2018; Maher, 2018; Ursu, 2018).

It is important to note the significance and benefits of the #MeToo movement. It has empowered survivors of sexual misconduct and their allies. It has resulted in diminished power and increased accountability for sexual predators and harassers. This has improved countless industries by, essentially, "cleaning house." The discussion that follows should not be interpreted as trying to downplay the #MeToo movement in any way.

POSSIBLE REACTIONS TO #METOO

The accusations and incidents of the #MeToo movement in literature lead to troublesome and difficult questions. Essentially, the questions boil down to this: What should we do about the books these authors have written and illustrators have illustrated?

Some of these books are on awards lists and/or bestseller lists. Some have been enjoyed for years by diverse patrons. Do we remove these books from circulation or place them in a special, restricted area? Should we plan to no longer purchase replacement copies or anything else connected to these authors and illustrators? Should we create some sort of warning label for these items? Or do we keep them on the shelves as if nothing has changed? What do we owe to our patrons, our coworkers, and ourselves?

These questions encompass several possible reactions and responses. Some have argued that we should remove the books from our libraries to avoid contributing to the accused's wealth, fame, and popularity.

Others have suggested placing the books in a restricted section (e.g., proverbially, behind the librarian's desk), requiring people to explicitly ask for them. Implicit in this suggestion is two ideas: few people would explicitly ask, and perhaps librarians could warn those who do. A similar idea is to add warning labels or some sort of cautionary tag to the books. Perhaps something could be written in the inside cover of a book, or a discreet but noticeable sticker could be attached to the outside of the cover.

While these approaches are well-meaning, they suffer from two fatal flaws. The latter two ideas try to impart a subtle, restricted access to the items in question. In other words, there is a perception that there is something negative about the books (because of the creators' actions), and both the restricted location and the cautionary warning try to impart that to the reader, with the hope that the books will be read less often (and, implicitly, weeded sooner). This is counter to intellectual freedom principles, which advocate for an open, freely accessible collection available without judgment of any sort.

Turning to Our Foundational Principles

More generally, however, all of these ideas are counter to intellectual freedom principles because they base judgment of an item on the actions of the author or contributor rather than on the content and merits of the *item itself.* This needs to be explored a bit further.

The first place to start is with our foundational values and principles. One of the core values of the American Library Association, of course, is intellectual freedom. The statement says, "We uphold the principles of intellectual freedom and *resist all efforts* to censor library resources" (ALA, 2006a, para. 8, emphasis added).

We can also turn to the Library Bill of Rights for guidance on complicated questions. Two precepts are particularly relevant here. The first principle says, "Materials should not be excluded because of the origin, background, or views of those contributing to their creation" (ALA, 2006c, para. 2) and the second principle states, "Libraries should provide materials and information presenting all points of view on current and historical issues. Materials should not be proscribed or removed because of partisan or doctrinal disapproval" (ALA, 2006c, para. 3). These two statements directly contradict the impulse to restrict access to books implicated in the #MeToo movement.

Next, we turn to the Freedom to Read Statement. The third proposition states,

> It is contrary to the public interest for publishers or librarians to bar access to writings on the basis of the personal history or political affiliations of the author. No art or literature can flourish if it is to be measured by the political views or private lives of its creators. (ALA, 2006b, para. 10)

This statement was originally written in 1953, during the communist scare in America. Writers who were actual or suspected communists were being blacklisted, and many librarians feared to purchase their books (and many librarians actually refused to collect books suspected of being connected to alleged communist authors).

With that background, it may seem a stretch to apply this statement to authors and illustrators implicated in the #MeToo movement. Yet "personal history" of authors clearly includes their sexual history, including allegations of predatory or harassing behavior. We can find such behavior despicable and repulsive, but it is not a fair or reasonable basis for evaluating these creators' works.

Taken together, these principles indicate that we should not remove the books of authors who have committed sexual misconduct or harassment. We would be removing books because of the background or personal history of the creators, which is explicitly opposed by our foundational core values and principles.

AN APPROACH INFORMED BY INTELLECTUAL FREEDOM

Instead of removing or restricting access to the items in question, we can approach these questions from an intellectual freedom perspective. This would be staying true to our foundational principles and values.

First, we can start by acknowledging that most libraries contain content that individual librarians (and patrons, of course) take issue with. For example, nearly every librarian, whether politically conservative, liberal, indifferent, or other, has selected and put on the shelves political books with which they disagree—and sometimes that disagreement is very strong. Both religious and nonreligious librarians regularly purchase and stock materials that cover a broad spectrum of religiosity and spirituality.

Disliking Items in the Library

While librarians rarely admit this, it is okay to dislike some items in your collection and on your shelves. That dislike can stem from many different sources: some librarians dislike certain illustrators' styles or perspectives; some librarians dislike romance, western, or other genres; some librarians are anti-LGBT and disapprove of selecting authors who identify as part of that community. There is a wide spectrum of reasons to dislike some of the items in your library—and some dislike is okay, even if it's rarely spoken about.

However, we *cannot* use that personal dislike to determine which books get added to or kept in a collection. A personal opinion is merely that— it is not a basis from which to make collection development decisions. Instead, as Chapter 7 noted, the collection development policy should be used as the foundation for which books to select and acquire (and, eventually, weed).

Most challenges to library items start as personal dislike: A patron reads a book (or simply hears about it), finds it objectionable, and wants to stop everyone else from having access to it. In response, libraries often state that individuals can make their own choices but cannot compel others to abide by those choices. This is the very heart of intellectual freedom.

If this principle applies to patrons, surely it should apply even more strongly to *librarians*, who have professional training in access to information and intellectual freedom principles.

Slippery Slope

Another important point is that libraries often contain materials created by authors whose conduct is offensive or even criminal. For example, there are numerous books written by actual, convicted criminals. Books have been written by people who've been publicly intoxicated, used and sold drugs, and so on. From minor crimes to serious felonies, many authors have admitted to crimes or been accused of criminal activity (even if not tried in a court of law).

If we say that authors who have committed sexual misconduct do not belong on our shelves, that will start a slippery slope. It will become difficult to include authors who have committed other crimes or, in some locales, those who have lived a nonconservative, nontraditional lifestyle. For example, rock stars who are promiscuous, use drugs, and tear up hotel rooms might be seen as poor role models and worthy of exclusion, not inclusion.

What about authors whose political or religious views are harmful to marginalized groups? These authors are often popular among certain patrons, and it would be a disservice to exclude books they want because of the authors' personal beliefs.

Indeed, librarians should not be in the business of drawing lines regarding what to exclude from their libraries. We focus on inclusion (in the words of Asheim [1953], we practice selection, not censorship). We evaluate a work on its *merits*, not on the personal beliefs or practices of its author.

Evaluating a Work on Its Merits

To evaluate a work on its merits, we should turn to the collection development policy, which should have explicit criteria for evaluating materials. We can ask if the books in question meet the criteria for remaining in the collection or continuing to be selected.

A useful example to consider is *The Absolutely True Diaries of a Part-Time Indian* by Sherman Alexie (from 2007). It's a book beloved by many and has received several awards. On the other hand, it's over a decade old now. Is it still circulating? Is it still relevant and meaningful to your patrons? For example, the book rarely discusses any technology, but today technology is a vital component of most teens' lives.

Are there other books out there that could portray growing up as an American Indian and/or growing up in poverty, with less-than-ideal home conditions, as a marginalized youth? In particular, since Alexie has been accused of quashing other American Indian voices (in addition to sexual misconduct), are there less well-known authors to whom you could give a boost? Different libraries may have different answers to these questions.

To approach these and other books from an intellectual freedom perspective, we must focus on *inclusion* rather than exclusion (or selection rather than censorship) and on the merits of the actual item rather than the actions of the author or illustrator.

WHAT ELSE CAN BE DONE?

In addition to fairly assessing the current merit of these items, there are other actions that your library can undertake. Perhaps this situation can lead to some relevant and timely programming.

Perhaps patrons would welcome an opportunity to discuss the implications of the #MeToo movement and how sexual misconduct, in any industry or profession, is horrible and creates myriad complications, ripples of pain, and difficulty that touch many of us in different ways. You could host a workshop (with appropriate mental health professionals) to discuss the implications of the #MeToo movement in literature and beyond.

This could also be a good opportunity to explain the principles of intellectual freedom to your patrons. Why would a library keep books by alleged harasser Alexie, for example? Such a decision may confuse patrons, so your library could have frank, thoughtful conversations about intellectual freedom and its role in the library, explaining that information access is a right. This could even have the benefit of reducing the number of challenges your library receives in the future.

Some libraries could host a creative writing group to write new stories, replacing the tarnished ones. Patrons, librarians, and others could collaborate to bolster the voices of survivors and accusers. Perhaps the library could then host a program on self-publishing or help the writers share their work in some way.

The library could also be deliberate about seeking out additional voices—especially voices from the #MeToo movement or voices that may have been quashed by perpetrators. Look for works by women and marginalized folks. Turn to smaller, alternative publishing companies that might specialize in bringing underrepresented voices to print.

Libraries might decide that they won't host or feature these authors and creators in programming. For example, James Dashner (author of

The Maze Runner) has been accused of sexual misconduct (Cohen & Hsu, 2018); libraries might decide they don't want to invite Dashner to their space, they don't want to feature his books in book clubs, and so on.

Another approach is to make one decision professionally and another personally. You may see that removing these books from the library is problematic, but at the same time, decide you will no longer support these authors in your personal life, ceasing to read anything they have written.

I see no problem with deciding, in one's personal life, that certain authors are now off-limits. The problem arises when someone tries to institute their personal beliefs over *all* library patrons.

CONCLUSION

This chapter explored some of the ramifications of the #MeToo movement for librarianship, specifically focusing on situations in which authors, illustrators, and others have been accused of sexual misconduct. We discussed various options for handling books by the accused but cautioned that many of these strategies would result in censorship of materials.

The better option, informed by intellectual freedom principles, is to evaluate items based on the library's collection development policy. This may result in some items remaining in the collection for some time, based on their popularity, condition, age, and so on. But any approach that limits access to these materials, especially when it's based on the background of the author, is antithetical to intellectual freedom.

We can now return to the anecdote at the beginning of the chapter: the children's books authored by Bill Cosby. Should they be kept in the library?

First, most of the books by Cosby are around twenty years old. Does your library routinely keep books of this age? Second, do the books still circulate and get use? Third, how relevant are they to the current generation of parents and kids? Fourth, are the books durable and in good shape? Fifth, consider the other parameters of your collection development policy and how they apply to the books in question. The goal here is not to find reasons to get rid of the books but to *fairly* assess their current value to the collection.

The librarians in this scenario carefully considered the above questions. When they ran circulation reports, they found that the Little Bill children's books did not circulate any longer, but *Love and Marriage* had recently circulated. Looking for additional information online, the librarians noted that the Little Bill series made to the list of the Top Ten Most Challenged Books in 2016 (ALA, 2013) because of the accusations against Cosby (which were later upheld in court). The books were in good condition (perhaps because of the lack of circulation). The librarians decided to not remove them immediately but to schedule the Little Bill books for removal during an upcoming weeding project.

REFERENCES

American Library Association. (2006a). Core values of librarianship. Retrieved from http://www.ala.org/advocacy/intfreedom/corevalues. Document ID: 33390955-19b0-2164-9d0d-07dfe5ec504e.

American Library Association. (2006b). Freedom to read statement. Retrieved from http://www.ala.org/advocacy/intfreedom/freedom readstatement. Document ID: aaac95d4-2988-0024-6573-10a5ce 6b21b2.

American Library Association. (2006c). Library bill of rights. Retrieved from http://www.ala.org/advocacy/intfreedom/librarybill. Document ID: 669fd6a3-8939-3e54-7577-996a0a3f8952.

American Library Association. (2013). Top ten most challenged books lists. Retrieved from http://www.ala.org/advocacy/bbooks/frequently challengedbooks/top10. Document ID: 8417fa9e-ceff-4512-aca9– 9fbc81b8bd81.

Asheim, L. (1953). Not censorship but selection. *Wilson Library Bulletin, 28*, 63–67.

Benshoff, L., & Allyn, B. (2018). Bill Cosby sentenced to at least three years in state prison for sexual assault. NPR. Retrieved from https://www.npr.org/2018/09/25/651065803/bill-cosby-sentenced-to-at-least-3-years-in-state-prison

Cohen, P., & Hsu, T. (2018). Children's book industry has its #MeToo moment. *New York Times*. Retrieved from https://www.nytimes.com/2018/02/15/business/childrens-publishing-sexual-harassment.html

Garcia, S.E. (2017). The woman who created #MeToo long before hashtags. *New York Times*. Retrieved from https://www.nytimes.com/2017/10/20/us/me-too-movement-tarana-burke.html

Framke, C. (2017). The sexual harassment allegations against Louis C.K., explained. Vox. Retrieved from https://www.vox.com/culture/2017/11/9/16629400/louis-ck-allegations-masturbation

Maher, J. (2018). Sexual harassment in children's publishing reaches a crisis point. *Publishers Weekly*. Retrieved from https://www.publishersweekly.com/pw/by-topic/childrens/childrens-industry-news/article/76049-sexual-harassment-in-children-s-publishing-comes-to-a-head.html

Ryzik, M. (2018). Louis C.K. performs first stand-up set at club since admitting to #MeToo cases. *New York Times*. Retrieved from https://www.nytimes.com/2018/08/27/arts/television/louis-ck-performs-comedy.html

Ryzik, M., Buckley, C., & Kantor, J. (2017). Louis C.K. is accused by 5 women of sexual misconduct. *New York Times*. Retrieved from https://www.nytimes.com/2017/11/09/arts/television/louis-ck-sexual-misconduct.html

Ursu, A. (2018). Sexual harassment in the children's book industry. Medium. Retrieved from https://medium.com/@anneursu_10179/sexual-harassment-in-the-childrens-book-industry-3417048ccde2

NINE

Programs, Meeting Rooms, and Exhibit Spaces

In libraries, programming means events or activities planned and hosted by the library staff. Outside speakers or entertainers may or may not be a part of the program. Many programs are interactive, such as storytimes that ask little ones to join in songs or crafting activities.

Although many people think of programming primarily in relation to public libraries, all types of libraries can host activities and events. For example, a school library may host a parent and guardian night to introduce caretakers to the resources of a modern school library media center. Academic libraries may host events to welcome international students or highlight some of the research being done with their collections. Special libraries may provide an event that showcases new resources or teaches patrons how to use parts of the collection. All types of libraries can host programming, which means that all types of libraries are susceptible to challenges to their programming events.

Likewise, many libraries of all types have meeting rooms available for their patrons to use. In this discussion, a meeting room in a library is a space that the library allows others to use to hold a meeting of some kind (such rooms usually have a door that can close, tables and chairs, and perhaps some technological equipment). Often a reservation is needed (and, for some libraries or some spaces, a small fee, though the American Library Association [ALA] discourages the use of fees). Some libraries have faced scrutiny and criticism from their patrons because of the groups that used the meeting rooms.

Libraries may also have exhibit spaces, community bulletin boards, displays, and so on in their facilities. While some of these spaces are designated only for staff use (e.g., putting up a display of recent fiction), they are all publicly viewable or accessible spaces for patrons. Perhaps surprisingly, many of these spaces have been subject to intellectual freedom challenges.

All of these types of spaces in libraries have been subject to challenges or criticism from patrons and others in the community. This chapter examines why programming, meeting rooms, and exhibit spaces may be challenged and the responses that librarians can make within an intellectual freedom context.

A recent example from 2018 exemplifies the intellectual freedom problems that libraries may encounter with programming. In O'Fallon, Illinois, the public library hosted a storytime centered around the children's book *Justice Makes a Difference* by Dr. Artika Tyner. The advertisement for the event said, "Using fun games and activities we will explore ideas of justice and social responsibility" (Venhaus, 2018).

A local conservative group raised concern about the event, claiming it was trying to indoctrinate children into caring about social justice. The group felt the library's event was not neutral.

What should the library do in this case? How can and should the library respond? Should the library have even held this event? How can the library avoid controversy in the future?

THE CONTENT OF PROGRAMMING

Generally, the objections to a library's programming are due to the content: some patrons object to whatever the programming is about. A program about the "fantastic beasts" of the Harry Potter world, for example, could draw complaints about an emphasis on magic and mythological creatures.

Often, challenged programming has a focus on marginalized groups, such as a poetry night featuring Latino writers. Sometimes the concern is that library resources are supporting a particular program, which can be seen, by patrons, as an endorsement of the content. The ALA explains,

> Library sponsorship of a program does not constitute an endorsement of the program content or the views expressed by the participants or speakers, any more than the purchase of material for the

library collection constitutes an endorsement of the material content or its creator's views. (2006b, para. 6)

Many patrons do not understand or realize that libraries are neutral with respect to content. This means the library does not endorse whatever content is a part of the programming. It is merely offered as an informational or recreational opportunity for patrons.

This is an educational opportunity—librarians can share the basics of intellectual freedom with their patrons and explain that the library is only offering a program, not endorsing its content. We can tie this back to our stance on books, explaining that we offer a wide diversity of viewpoints in books and in other formats, including programming. (Of course, this assumes that libraries *are* offering varied, diverse programming.)

Libraries should take care that the content of the programming is supported, whenever possible, by materials and resources available in the library. The aforementioned Latino poetry night, for instance, could be accompanied by a display of relevant writers, films, and music. In pulling related content, librarians should be sure they are representing diverse perspectives. Thus, an event about voter registration could be tied to the political books the library holds, but this should only be done if the library displays books across the political spectrum.

Making these connections between the collection and the program is useful because it provides a foundation for the program; if the library thought the content was important enough to collect resources on, then it seems justifiable to also host a program. Conversely, if a topic is interesting or important enough for a program, then the library will probably want to ensure it has resources to support that interest.

Libraries also need to consider the neutrality or impartiality of their programming. Because of libraries' stance on intellectual freedom, these institutions cannot endorse political candidates or positions, support certain religions, or choose sides on other divisive topics. Many libraries (school libraries, most public libraries, some academic libraries, and a few special libraries) are supported by tax dollars, which means they cannot endorse a political candidate or stance.

Thus, the voter registration event described previously would be politically neutral, but having a speaker who argued Republicans were trying to suppress voter turnout would not be neutral. A few considerations can be particularly helpful here.

First, consider the library's mission statement. Does it include words like "inform," "educate," and "entertain"? And does the content of the proposed programming actually inform, educate, or entertain? Patrons should be able to see a connection between what the library does (in its programming, for instance) and what the library purports to be about (in its mission statement). At the same time, the library should interpret the mission statement broadly and be inclusive of diverse, creative programming.

Second, consider crafting a policy about library programming. This policy should emphasize the importance of both intellectual freedom and neutrality. The ALA suggests that such a policy should mirror the collection development policy and should refer to the Library Bill of Rights, emphasizing patrons' right to access information (in all forms) (ALA, 2006a).

Third, carefully plan the content of the programming. If an outside speaker is coming into the library, having an outline of what he or she intends to say could be helpful. The intent here is *not* to censor the speaker but to ensure that his or her plans follow the library's policy and mission statement.

WHEN PROGRAMMING GETS CHALLENGED

Despite taking these steps, library programming may still be challenged by patrons who are upset with its content or message. As with materials challenges, the basic approach is to remain calm and listen to the challenger. Often, people just want to air grievance and don't have a desire to push things further or file formal paperwork.

It is helpful to have a library policy about how to handle challenges to programming. This can be similar (or even the same) as the policy about how to handle materials challenges. The goal here is not to craft countless policies covering any potential incident; instead, the goal is to have a thoughtful plan in place that can be implemented if the need arises. Letting challengers know there is an impartial policy and plan can help calm them down as well. This tells challengers you take their concerns seriously.

From here, you can follow the same procedures as you would for a challenge to library resources: have a committee review the content and make a determination (see Chapter 6). This committee may consider whether the library has other materials related to the content of the programming, whether other libraries have hosted similar events, whether similar programming is addressed in the professional literature, and whether the event aligns with the library's mission statement.

The committee may decide that the content of the programming was fine, in which case no further action needs to be taken (other than notifying the challenger). If the committee decides the programming was inappropriate, then the library may need to review its process for determining the content of programming and approving it.

MEETING ROOM CHALLENGES

Because meeting rooms are visible and/or accessible by the library's patrons, patrons are likely to consider them representative of the library in some way. Along these lines, patrons may think that allowing a group to use the meeting room carries a connotation (to patrons) that the library condones that group. Patrons may think that the library would simply ban groups it did not like.

Since some patrons have this belief, conflicts arise: if the patron doesn't like a group that is using the meeting room, that patron will likely be upset with the library just as much as with the problematic group (if not more).

For example, in the past, some public libraries have allowed white pride groups (Foskett, 2011) and anti-immigration groups (Price & Glover, 2012) to use their meeting rooms. In both cases, these meetings sparked controversy and counter-protests, as patrons seemed to think that the libraries should refuse to let these groups use the rooms.

Of course, this reveals a fundamental misunderstanding of most library mission statements and core beliefs. As we've discussed in previous chapters, libraries contain a broad diversity of information resources, regardless of whether individual librarians approve of them. The same holds true for meeting rooms—the access is made available to *all*, regardless of whether librarians approve of them.

In its meeting room interpretation of the Library Bill of Rights, the ALA says, "Libraries may wish to post a permanent notice near the meeting room stating that the library does not advocate or endorse the viewpoints of meetings or meeting room users" (ALA, 2006b, para. 3). This would clarify, for patrons, that libraries are neutral with respect to the content and purpose of meeting rooms.

Sometimes this principle gets tested. A few years ago, some citizens in northern Kentucky challenged the way that taxation for public libraries was determined, which could have resulted in local libraries' closure (see Warburton, 2015, for more details). The citizens in question needed to meet to plan their strategy and write their lawsuit, so they used the local library's meeting rooms (J.C. Morgan, personal communication, 2018).

Other patrons found it ironic that this group, whose lawsuit would result in the closure of libraries, would rely on library meeting rooms. The library in question had no comment. They simply opened the meeting room as they would for any other group. This is a great example of just how seriously libraries take the neutrality principle.

According to this principle, meeting rooms may be used for a variety of reasons and by a variety of groups. Principle six of the Library Bill of Rights says that libraries "should make such facilities available on an equitable basis, regardless of the beliefs or affiliations of individuals or groups requesting their use" (ALA, 2006a, para. 7). This means that libraries cannot ban groups with whom they disagree.

Meeting Room Policies

Libraries often have policies about the ways in which their meeting rooms can or cannot be used. It is a good idea to have a formal written policy to use to guide staff actions; it can also be used to address patron concerns or questions. Policies for meeting rooms should be written based on guidance from the ALA, from your state library association, and in conjunction with an attorney, who will be able to ensure that the policy is in line with relevant judicial opinions.

Sometimes these policies are written with the best of intentions, yet they inadvertently violate established law. For example, many public libraries state that religious worship cannot be held in their meeting rooms, but courts have consistently ruled that public libraries cannot ban religious activities. Worship (including singing hymns) should be included in "religious activities" (ALA, 2010).

There are some generally accepted guidelines for meeting room policies. Usually, whoever is hosting the meeting must allow all interested parties to attend. In other words, libraries can ban meetings with restricted access since libraries function to provide access to all. This may have the practical effect of discouraging some political or religious groups from using library meeting rooms.

It is also acceptable to limit meeting room access to your usual patrons or community. Thus, an academic library might have a policy that only students, staff, and faculty of the university can utilize the meeting rooms.

Currently, the ALA is revising its policy regarding meeting rooms. In 2018, the organization updated the meeting room policy and included language explicitly indicating that libraries could not ban "hate groups." This caused an uproar, as many felt this language was insensitive to those who were targets of hate groups *and* likely to encourage hate groups to patronize libraries. Neither of those was a desirable outcome.

In the fall of 2018, this language was rescinded, and the policy underwent further rounds of revision and comment. To see the latest version of the official policy, you can search for it on ALA's website.

If a patron is upset about the use of the library's meeting rooms, the response should be similar to other situations that involve an upset patron. Listen to the patron respectfully, and note their concerns. Try to explain the library's stance on intellectual freedom and neutrality. Explain that all patrons have the right to use the meeting rooms and the library does not restrict access, but the library also does not support or condone whoever is using the meeting rooms.

Depending on the situation, you could suggest that the patron hold a counter-balancing meeting. For example, to counter an anti-immigration meeting, perhaps a concerned patron could hold a meeting to discuss ways to demonstrate support of immigrants.

DISPLAYS, EXHIBIT SPACES, AND BULLETIN BOARDS

In some ways, the concerns about displays, exhibit spaces, and bulletin boards are similar to the concerns about meeting rooms or programming. These are publicly viewable and accessible spaces, and patrons may think that the library is indicating approval or support of whatever is posted or displayed.

Displays are generally created by library staff to highlight items in the library collection. Similar to the previous discussion, if a patron thinks the library approves of all books in a display, but the patron disapproves of them, then the patron will object to the display. For example, a book display in February might focus on romance; it might include films with an interracial relationship or books that include premarital sex. Patrons who disapprove of these lifestyles could be upset that the library appears to promote these materials.

Exhibit Spaces

Exhibit spaces are locations where nonlibrary staff are allowed (and sometimes encouraged) to post information or displays. For example, an exhibit space may be a large glassed bookshelf used to display items. Perhaps the local Women's Society wants to display items related to traditional female crafts, such as knitting and embroidery.

Sometimes these spaces are not made available to patrons for their use. If they are, however, access must be given equitably. This is another time that a policy governing use and access is a good idea.

Another type of exhibit space is an area where local free newspapers or other publications are available to patrons. Generally located at the front of the library, these spaces are available for community publications, alternative weeklies, and other similar publications to be distributed for free to the community. Usually, libraries do not govern or monitor the content of these publications.

In Las Vegas, a public library recently made news when a patron complained about the content of a gay lifestyle magazine freely available in the lobby area of the library (Ortiz, 2018). The library's response is worth quoting in full because of the robust intellectual freedom stance it takes:

> The Library District collects, gathers, and makes available a wide variety of information and we understand that some people may occasionally find these materials offensive or inappropriate. The public library is a First Amendment public institution.
>
> Yes, the Library District is aware of various magazines that are displayed in our lobbies. Our Display Policy, adopted by the Library Board in 1999, allows for free community-based publications that contain news and feature articles relevant to either segments of a district-wide population or to smaller geographic areas within the Library District to be circulated.
>
> The presence of these materials in the Library District is not a form of endorsement. We encourage individuals to form their own opinion about what they choose the read or view. (Ortiz, 2018, para. 8–10)

This approach is commendable for a few reasons. First, the library has a formal policy that it uses to guide its approach to such publications and to patron concern. This avoids inflammatory or reactive responses. Second, the policy emphasizes gathering information that is relevant to parts of their community, always an important approach for libraries. Third, the policy notes that the library merely makes the information available, without endorsing it. Taken together, these provide a strong response grounded in intellectual freedom.

Community Bulletin Boards

Another type of community space found in many libraries is community bulletin boards, which are generally spaces where members of the community can post fliers and advertisements to share with other members of the community.

It can be quite difficult to write usage policies for these spaces. Generally, prohibiting images or items can be difficult because of the intellectual freedom orientations of libraries. A library may wish to ban items or fliers that are in "poor taste" or do not meet community standards.

However, there is no accepted definition of poor taste or community standards. These can actually vary quite a bit depending on which part of the community one focuses upon. Some community members may not want to see a flier about a pagan religious event, while others would be delighted to learn such information, for example. Local and state ordinances about appropriate content (e.g., barring profanity) could be useful in these situations.

One limitation that often seems reasonable is limiting content based on the type of library. For example, a fine arts library at a university may only allow arts-related fliers on its community board. A school library may only allow information pertaining to the education of its students. For public libraries, however, this exception would be quite limited.

AN INTELLECTUAL FREEDOM FOUNDATION

Each of these types of spaces—meeting rooms, programs, displays, exhibits, and community bulletin boards—face similar dilemmas. Because they are publicly accessible and viewable spaces, patrons may take the views presented there as representative of the library. Even when some patrons create or contribute to the content, others may not realize this and may still attribute it to the library.

Making these spaces accessible and sharing control over the content (e.g., of community bulletin boards) are important ways to further intellectual freedom in libraries. These spaces can provide more information and resources for patrons, thus improving their access to information. These spaces can also allow patrons to express themselves (particularly meeting rooms, some programming, exhibit spaces, and community bulletin boards), which allows them to utilize their freedom of speech.

Even if it is the library using these spaces (as opposed to patron-created content), doing so still arguably improves intellectual freedom. From a position informed by intellectual freedom, creating a display, posting something on a bulletin board, or opening a meeting room are all ways to demonstrate neutrality and share resources rather than put an implicit stamp of approval on them.

It's clear that not all patrons know about or understand this stance, however, so it needs to be an area of ongoing education and communication. Again, putting up a notice that explicitly states the library does not endorse the content (of the bulletin board, of the meeting room, etc.) can be a helpful explanation for patrons. Occasional programming that explains and discusses intellectual freedom would be helpful as well and would likely gain the library more supporters.

CONCLUSION

In this chapter, we have discussed some of the "other" spaces of libraries (i.e., other spaces beyond stacks of books and rows of computers). These spaces include meeting rooms, programming events, displays, exhibit spaces, and community bulletin boards. While there are many differences between these spaces, they are all publicly viewable or accessible (and, in many of them, patrons can create or contribute content).

Just like other areas of a library, these spaces should be viewed from an intellectual freedom perspective. They offer important freedom of speech opportunities to patrons—spaces both to access information and to express ourselves. They are also spaces in which libraries demonstrate the principle of neutrality, offering access to information without endorsing it. These are fundamental components of intellectual freedom, though they may need to be explained to patrons who express concern.

This is what happened in the public library in Illinois, mentioned at the beginning of this chapter. The library had hosted a storytime focused on a particular book, with crafts and activities, all centered around the theme of "social justice."

While over twenty children and their parents attended the storytime and participated, some community members were upset with the theme. These community members thought that an event focused on "social justice" was a form of indoctrination, and they raised concern in city council meetings.

The public library noted that this storytime was a popular event and was not an endorsement of one perspective or another. Instead, it focused on how participants could be engaged members of their own communities. The unrest faded away after a few weeks, in part because many community members rallied to the library's defense. They understood that the library was not endorsing a viewpoint but offering access to information and resources.

REFERENCES

American Library Association. (2006a). Library bill of rights. Retrieved from http://www.ala.org/advocacy/intfreedom/librarybill. Document ID: 669fd6a3-8939-3e54–7577-996a0a3f8952.

American Library Association. (2006b). Library-initiated programs as a resource: An interpretation of the library bill of rights. Retrieved from http://www.ala.org/advocacy/intfreedom/librarybill/interpretations/programs. Document ID: 94f556e1-b954-aaa4-d99d-2f42a0177754.

American Library Association. (2010). Religion in American libraries: Questions and answers. Retrieved from http://www.ala.org/advocacy/intfreedom/religionFAQ. Document ID: a771bca0-e719-b544-e522-3b26c50eb338.

Foskett, S. H., Jr. (2011). Library declines to change rules after white pride controversy. Telegram.com. Retrieved from https://www.telegram.com/article/20110913/NEWS/110919840

Ortiz, A. (2018). Parents upset over racy magazines in Las Vegas public libraries. *13 Action News*. Retrieved from https://www.ktnv.com/news/racy-magazine-found-at-public-library

Price, B., & Glover, J. (2012). Protest held outside anti-immigrant meeting at Boone County Library. WCPO Cincinnati. Retrieved from https://www.wcpo.com/news/protests-planned-outside-anti-immigrant-meeting-at-boone-county-library-in-union

Venhaus, L. (2018). O'Fallon library children's book choice was "indoctrination," conservative group says. *Belleville News-Democrat*. Retrieved from https://www.bnd.com/news/local/community/ofallon-progress/article209980034.html

Warburton, B. (2015). KY appeals court: Library taxes legal. *Library Journal*. Retrieved from https://www.libraryjournal.com/?detailStory=ky-appeals-court-library-taxes-legal

TEN

Internet Filtering

This chapter explains internet filtering and its connection to intellectual freedom. While many people view internet filtering as a positive way to reduce access to inappropriate content on the internet, the issues are actually more complex.

For example, students on debate teams may not be able to access content needed to write their arguments on topics such as climate change, drug addiction, gun control, intimate partner violence, or other complicated issues. Some critical information (from more than one perspective) would likely be blocked by many of the internet filters used in schools.

Many lesbian, gay, bisexual, and transgender (LGBT) sites are blocked by internet filters, including anti-bullying sites such as It Gets Better. This is a site designed to instill hope in those who are bullied or who just don't fit in at their schools, but because it has LGBT content, it gets lumped in with other queer content sites and gets blocked.

There are clear implications for freedom of speech and the right to receive information when it comes to internet filters. Although internet filtering occurs most often in schools and public libraries, academic and special libraries may encounter these issues as well.

Imagine a teen growing up in a home that supports white supremacist ideology and denigrates people of other races. But he encounters people of color at school and begins to doubt his family's ideology. Where can he turn? One option might be the public library. When this happened in a rural midwestern town, the teen in question tried finding anti-hate sites at the public library, looking for information that might debunk the ideology he had been taught by his family. Unfortunately, these sites were blocked by the internet filter. The filter was set to block white supremacy sites, and since anti-supremacy sites used similar vocabulary, they were blocked as well.

What should the library do in this case? If it's possible, should the internet filter be temporarily disabled for the computer the teen is using? Should these sites continue to be blocked? What power does the library have in this situation? What *responsibility* does the library have? We will explore the complexities of internet filtering next and then return to these questions.

DEFINING INTERNET FILTERING

The National Coalition Against Censorship (NCAC) defines "internet filters" as "software that prevents users of a computer from accessing certain websites" (n.d., para. 1). Essentially, the software acts as a filter, allowing some information to pass through while blocking other information or websites. Which websites are allowed or blocked varies greatly— and is the source for much concern about internet filters.

Most internet filters use algorithms to determine which websites are blocked (blacklisted) or allowed (whitelisted). Nearly all internet filters are commercial products, meaning that their algorithms for determining black or white lists are proprietary and not available to the general public (or librarians) or to the institutions using their software.

In other words, the software makes a determination about particular websites, but the users of the software (and the general public) do not get to know the process behind that decision. Furthermore, the people making these decisions are generally computer scientists or engineers, not librarians or others who have strong regard for the First Amendment right to access information.

In addition, many internet filtering companies offer to block *categories* of information (as opposed to blocking a list of websites, which is often not very effective). These categories (and their content) vary widely among the different software companies. For example, categories might include "adult/mature content," "illegal drugs," and "pornography," as well as "arts/entertainment," "LGBT," and "society/daily living." Researchers recently studied the deployment of internet filtering in Alabama (Peterson, Oltmann, & Knox, 2017), and their paper contains some examples of these different categories.

Typically, an institution using the software can identify which categories of information it would like to have blacklisted, and then the software does its best to allow no websites in those categories to be accessed by users. However, the specific content of each category (exactly which websites are included) are proprietary information and thus not shared with librarians or the general public.

This may be particularly problematic when it comes to content areas that are controversial or disliked by certain groups of people. In Missouri in 2013, a patron filed suit because her local public library blocked access to sites about paganism and Native American religions. The librarian in that situation felt that these sites were not necessary and provided no information that anyone in her county would need. The lawsuit was settled once the library changed its policies and allowed those sites to be accessed (Patrick, 2013). This case shows that people disagree about what should be blocked by internet filters.

In addition to concern about which content categories are blocked, there is legitimate concern about which websites are included in each category. For example, in the "LGBT" category, websites might include images of gay pride festivals and parades, safer sex practices for same-sex couples, anti-bullying and anti-harassment campaigns, erotica and pornography, and many other types of information. Because it all concerns the LGBT community in some way, though, it will all be indiscriminately blocked. It seems commonsense to note that much of that information is not harmful but in fact could be helpful to many people.

The category of "illegal drugs" contains not only information about these drugs and information about their effects but also antidrug education and sites about "kicking the habit." Some categories are even more ambiguous. It is not clear what "society/daily living" means or which sites would be included in this category—or why they would need to be blocked.

CHILDREN'S INTERNET PROTECTION ACT

When discussing internet filtering, we must also discuss the Children's Internet Protection Act (CIPA) because this law ties internet filtering to certain types of federal funding (called "E-rate discounts," used to discount pricing on telecommunications and internet access).

Schools and public libraries that receive this funding are required by law to install and use an internet filter; this must be recertified and documented each year. CIPA requires that all computers in an institution be filtered; thus, even adult-only computers (as well as staff computers) must have filters to be compliant with the law.

According to CIPA, these filters must be used to block visual depictions that are obscene, child pornography, or "harmful to minors." The categories of "obscene" and "child pornography" have been legally defined by the court system and are illegal in the United States. The phrase "harmful to minors" was newly introduced in the law and encompasses

> any picture, image, graphic image file, or other visual depiction that—(i) taken as a whole and with respect to minors, appeals to a prurient interest in nudity, sex, or excretion; (ii) depicts, describes, or represents, in a patently offensive way with respect to what is suitable for minors, an actual or simulated sexual act or sexual contact, actual or simulated normal or perverted sexual acts, or a lewd exhibition of the genitals; and (iii) taken as a whole, lacks serious literary, artistic, political, or scientific value as to minors. (Title XVII, Sec. 1703, para. 10–12)

Material that could be considered "harmful to minors" includes much *constitutionally protected speech*. Only a few categories of speech (e.g., obscenity, child pornography, and slander) are not protected by the First Amendment; thus, nearly everything described in the definition of "harmful to minors" would fall under First Amendment protection.

A good example is nudity, including nude statues and artwork. It could easily be argued that nude artwork "appeals to a prurient interest" or contains a "lewd exhibition of the genitals." Many internet filters would block access to nude images. At the same time, however, much important Renaissance and Romantic art includes nudity. To study art history, one would need to be able to access these images (as well as writing about them). Just as clearly, nude artwork is protected by the First Amendment. This is a case where the First Amendment protects certain speech, yet CIPA tries to prevent access to it.

Due to the concern that CIPA required schools and libraries to filter legal content, the American Library Association (ALA) filed suit to block implementation of the law. In 2003, the ALA lost its case at the Supreme Court, and thus, CIPA has been enforced since that time (*United States v. American Library Association*, 2003).

This means that every school system and public library system that receives E-rate federal funds must install an internet filter and block information that is obscene, child pornography, and harmful to minors.

In practice, this means that virtually all school systems and many public libraries do use internet filters (though there are no reliable statistics about the exact proportion of institutions that use internet filters).

In some cases, the internet filter can be temporarily removed or turned off. According to CIPA, if an adult is conducting "bona fide research," and needs access to a blocked site, he or she can request that the filter be temporarily removed. CIPA does not, however, define or explain "bona fide research," and some library directors have been known to refuse such requests (Oltmann, 2016). Klinefelter (2010) notes, though, that the ability to make such requests was seen as essential by eight of the Supreme Court justices when deciding the CIPA lawsuit. When an adult desires or requires an unfiltered internet, but is denied, this can be seen as another problem with internet filtering.

PROBLEMS WITH INTERNET FILTERING

There are two concerns with internet filtering that are frequently mentioned: overblocking and underblocking. As the term suggests, "overblocking" means that the internet filter is blocking more content than it should. A classic example is that filters could be set to block anything about "breasts," in an attempt to limit access to pornography; however, this could end up blocking sites about chicken breasts or breast cancer. This information could be needed for research or health purposes (or just for recreation, such as recipes that include chicken breasts).

Internet filters have become more sophisticated and nuanced over time, meaning that such mistakes are less likely today. However, the differences between a sex education site and a pornographic site are subtler and therefore still likely to result in overblocking.

In contrast, "underblocking" means that the internet filter does not catch and block everything in a particular category. This can often happen with sites that are primarily image-based or video-based (as opposed to text-based), because images and videos are more difficult to categorize.

Other Subtler Problems with Internet Filtering

A subtler problem with internet filtering is the way it takes responsibility out of users' hands. When the internet is unfiltered, users are subjected to an incredibly broad swathe of information, some of which is poorly researched, poorly written, inappropriate, controversial, or just plain wrong. The internet has been called a "digital wild west," and we can often understand why.

Users must evaluate different sites and practice digital citizenship skills to avoid accessing sites they should not. This involves educating and training users about appropriate information and using discernment and reasoning to evaluate the resources they find online (see Chapter 11 for a deeper exploration of this issue).

However, when the internet is filtered, people lose the opportunity to learn, practice, and hone these skills. They may not learn how to be a good digital user of information around others, respecting public space. Users will be less likely to develop the digital literacy skills of evaluating and weeding out inappropriate information.

Another problem with internet filters has to do with how they are installed and used. To comply with CIPA, all computers in an institution must have filters. This means no distinction is made between toddlers, juveniles, teens, and even adults. Though the maturity level, information needs, and ability to handle complex information vary widely between these groups, according to CIPA, no differentiation in filtering is allowed. Thus, it may seem reasonable to prevent a seven-year-old from accessing a sex education site, but what about a seventeen-year-old? Or an adult? (There is also no distinction made for staff computers, which, by law, must be filtered.)

As you can see, the categories discussed earlier (such as "LGBT," "illegal drugs," and "society/daily living") do not map neatly onto the category of "harmful to minors" that the law requires. In fact, there is no simple correlation between the legally required categories and the categories that most internet filters offer to block.

This means that different institutions may decide that different categories are "harmful to minors." Access to information on the internet can thus vary from location to location. One library, for example, might opt to have "illegal drugs" and "society/daily living" blocked from its computers, while another library (sometimes in the next county over!) allows those categories. As Peterson et al. (2017) show, this results in highly variable access to the internet, and the variance is determined by, typically, library directors or administrators. In other words, sometimes a single person makes a decision about which information can be accessed online by anyone who uses the institution, which is then enforced by the internet filter.

This brings up, once again, the *subjectivity* of deciding which information people should be allowed to access. The legal guideline of what people should be allowed to access is the First Amendment, which permits and protects access to virtually all information (except for a few categories, described previously). With CIPA, a new legal guideline was introduced: harmful to minors.

Though a long definition of this phrase was included in the law, it is still a subjective phrase. Each person's understanding of "harmful to minors" is likely to vary. Some people may believe that access to any information that references the LGBT community is harmful. Others may believe that access to positive images like gay pride parades or positive sites like anti-bullying pages is beneficial to many youth (both straight and LGBT). Similar arguments can be made for any of the categories of information that internet filters offer to block (with the exception of non-protected speech like obscenity).

As we established in Part I of the book, intellectual freedom is about protecting and enhancing access to information (see especially Chapters 1 and 2). The ALA defines "intellectual freedom" as

> Intellectual freedom is the right of every individual to both seek and receive information from all points of view without restriction. It provides for free access to all expressions of ideas through which any and all sides of a question, cause or movement may be explored. (ALA, 2007)

Recall that access to information or receiving information is part of the First Amendment protection for freedom of speech. In contrast, internet filtering inherently *limits* access to information. Internet filtering explicitly tries to block access to "any and all sides of a question, cause or movement."

WHAT CAN BE DONE ABOUT INTERNET FILTERING

Given these problems with internet filtering, what can be done? There are several ways to tackle the problem of internet filtering and reduce its negative impact on information access.

First, we have to acknowledge the realities of the contemporary age: internet filtering is not going to go away. Especially in schools, where most patrons are minors, internet filtering will likely remain the standard, not the exception.

Having said that, other types of institutions can and should *thoughtfully* examine whether internet filtering is a good fit for them. CIPA only applies to schools and public libraries, so other types of information organizations (e.g., academic libraries, special libraries, archives, and medical libraries) do not legally need internet filters. They should consider whether internet filtering aids or hinders their mission and is appropriate for their patron base.

Public libraries likewise should consider whether use of internet filtering is necessary and appropriate for their communities. In some locales, libraries feel compelled to use internet filters because they would not be able to supply internet access without using the E-rate discount that is tied to filtering.

However, in other locales, public libraries have been able to convince their communities to raise taxes slightly to cover the difference that E-rates would make; this means that those libraries can provide internet access without using internet filters. Every library should consider whether this is a possibility, through discussions with the board of trustees and community members.

The Least Restrictive Approach

If having no filters is not an option, then the institution should use a *least restrictive*[1] approach. What is the least restrictive internet filter available in the area? How much information is the filtering company willing to share about its underlying philosophy and practices? For example, is the company explicitly Christian, and if so, does that affect which sites gets whitelisted or blacklisted? Any company unwilling to share its basic philosophical approach to filtering (not its algorithms) should be viewed with serious caution.

Information organizations should also think carefully about which categories of content they decide to have blocked. For example, do "society/daily living" sites really need to be blacklisted in your particular institution? What is the potential harm of allowing access? In most cases, the harm would be minimal or nonexistent. Each category should be thoughtfully reviewed. It would be helpful to know the full extent of what is included in each category, though most internet filtering companies will not reveal this information.

Instead, you should consider what could be included in a very broad conceptualization of the category—look at the likely blocked sites in an LGBT category aforementioned, as an example. Weigh the advantages and disadvantages of blocking access to this broad swathe of information. It may be true that much of the information that can be blocked by this categorical approach is not educational. Perhaps it is purely recreational or pleasurable, but so are *many* of the resources in a library. This may be a good time to review the library's mission statement and consider whether blocking certain categories is really congruent with the library's mission in the community.

Internet filtering is often subscribed to or paid for at the system or consortia level; sometimes there are statewide resources available. These should be viewed with the same caution as any other company, since information accessibility was probably not the primary consideration when the state-level or consortia-level filtering company was selected. Here, individual libraries can be advocates for access to information, arguing for the least restrictive approach (rather than the least costly approach, as often happens).

In addition to making sure that the least restrictive approach is taken, ensure that the filter can be removed upon request. Ideally, this would be enabled so that an employee at any customer service point can temporarily disable the filter, as opposed to waiting for an IT employee or someone at a regional branch to do so. There should be no or few hoops for a requestor to jump through—no paperwork, for example. He or she should not have to explain the need for unfiltered access beyond "research" (or "bona fide research" in the words of CIPA).

Make this process as painless and simple as possible; a requestor may be embarrassed or feel awkward about making this request, but our goal should be to minimize these feelings. As we have seen, even the best internet filters will block valuable, noncontroversial information, so libraries need to have straightforward processes to remove filters upon request.

CONCLUSION

Though many public libraries and nearly all schools use internet filtering, it is highly problematic from an intellectual freedom perspective. Internet filters essentially exist to reduce access to information. Although some of the information that is blocked may be banned by law (e.g., obscenity, child pornography, and content that is harmful to minors), much of the information that internet filters block is constitutionally protected speech. People have a right to access this information.

Because of this, libraries and similar institutions should think carefully about installing and using internet filters. Ideally, filters should be used in the least restrictive manner, blocking only what is absolutely necessary while allowing access to the broad swathe of information available online.

Let's return to the anecdote from the beginning of the chapter. In that situation, a teen wanted to access information challenging white supremacist ideology but was blocked by the library's internet filter. In this case, the library should allow the teen to access the information by temporarily disabling the internet filter; if that cannot be done, the library should investigate how to do so in the future. The library can also direct the teen to offline resources (perhaps there are some nonfiction books that would be helpful).

Finally, the library should consider unblocking this category of content. Although doing so would likely allow hate speech to be accessed in the library, it would *also* allow anti-hate speech to be accessed. Both perspectives are actually protected by the First Amendment and thus should be accessible to patrons.

NOTE

1. The phrase "least restrictive" is actually used by the Supreme Court with regard to some laws about freedom of speech. Essentially, a law that restricts some speech is constitutional only if it protects a compelling interest of the government and is the least restrictive means available (see Ruane, 2014, for a good explanation). I'm adopting this phrase here for internet filtering, though the Supreme Court hasn't used it in this way.

REFERENCES

American Library Association. (2007). Intellectual freedom and censorship Q&A. Retrieved from http://www.ala.org/advocacy/intfreedom/censorship/faq. Document ID: e8ae9ed7-a469-f0d4-adf0-f2770d2ca8e8.

Children's Internet Protection Act. (2000). 47 CFR § 54.520.

Klinefelter, A. (2010). First Amendment limits on library collection management. *Law Library Journal, 102*(3), 343–374.

National Coalition Against Censorship. (n.d.). Internet filters. Retrieved from https://ncac.org/resource/internet-filters-2

Oltmann, S. M. (2016). "For all the people": Public library directors interpret intellectual freedom. *Library Quarterly, 86*(3), 290–312.

Patrick, R. (2013). Missouri library agrees not to block witch websites. *St. Louis Post-Dispatch.* Retrieved from https://www.stltoday.com/

news/local/crime-and-courts/missouri-library-agrees-not-to-block-witch-websites/article_5f3ec8c8-b490-5479-a02d-4e7f2922e9d3.html

Peterson, C., Oltmann, S. M., & Knox, E. J. M. (2017). The inconsistent work of web filters: Mapping information access in Alabama public schools and libraries. *International Journal of Communication, 11.* Retrieved from https://ijoc.org/index.php/ijoc/article/view/6944

Ruane, K. A. (2014). *Freedom of speech and press: Exceptions to the First Amendment.* Congressional Research Service. Report #95–815.

United States v. American Library Association, 539 U.S. 194 (2003).

ELEVEN

Fake News, False Information, and Intellectual Freedom

Fake news, misinformation, disinformation, and related homonyms are frequently used in the media these days—and are increasingly common in library and information science. At the root of this increased attention is concern that some people are deliberately creating and spreading false news for myriad reasons—but often to confuse others and sow disagreement.

A related concern is that people may not be able to differentiate between accurate and inaccurate information, especially because false information is increasingly sophisticated. This can affect all areas of a person's life, though we see fake news perhaps most frequently in health information and politics.

To illustrate the complexity of false information, we can consider the book *Arming America: The Origins of a National Gun Culture*, written in 2000 by Michael A. Bellesiles. This book initially garnered positive reviews and even won the prestigious Bancroft Prize (given to books about diplomacy or the history of the Americas). Many academic and public libraries purchased the book.

However, its claims were soon called into question. Other historians noted fabrications, falsehoods, and problems with citations (see McLemee, 2010, for a summary). The controversy led the prize committee to rescind the Bancroft Prize and Bellesiles to resign from Emory University.

Libraries then faced a quandary: What should they do with this book? Did it still have a place on their shelves? More generally, what should librarians do in the face of false information? What does an intellectual freedom lens offer with regard to false information?

WHAT IS FALSE INFORMATION?

Some phrases are politically charged, such as "fake news." Using the term "fake news" may turn off some people before any discussion even begins, so this chapter will avoid that particular phrase and use "false information" instead.

Researchers often distinguish between different types of false information. These types include misinformation, disinformation, missing information, and outright ignorance (Froehlich, 2017). Misinformation and disinformation are most relevant to our discussion.

Cooke (2018) defines "misinformation" as information that is "incomplete . . . but [it] can also be categorized as information that is uncertain, vague, or ambiguous" (p. 38). Generally, misinformation is not true, but there is not a deliberate intention to mislead others.

In contrast, disinformation is false information that is *deliberately* false and knowingly disseminated—there is a purposeful intention to mislead others (Cooke, 2018; Froehlich, 2017). "Fake news" is a subset of disinformation. It is created to deliberately mislead others about news and current events.

Here, we will use "false information" as a more neutral term for information that is demonstrably not true. This encompasses both disinformation and misinformation. Despite its lack of veracity, false information may spread quickly and persistently (defeating attempts to rebut it). In fact, research has found that false information can spread *more* quickly and farther than factual information (Vosoughi, Roy, & Aral, 2018).

Many people may feel they know false information when they see it, but this is probably just a comforting thought. In reality, quite a few of us have been taken in, at least briefly, by false information, rumors, and hoaxes, particularly online (Wood, 2018).

In addition to the above definition of disinformation, we can point to some frequent characteristics of false information. One characteristic of false information in our contemporary age is that it seems to thrive online, often shared through various social media channels. Through social media, false information can spread incredibly quickly. In addition, social media makes it easy to share information but not as easy to double-check sources, refer to the original creator, or fact-check information.

Another important characteristic of false information is that it generally seems believable, at least to some people. It may contain an element of truth or start with some truth and then veer into falsehood.

Relatedly, false news is increasingly sophisticated and well-produced. In fact, researchers have demonstrated they can use artificial intelligence to create fake videos that are so convincing that most people cannot tell the fake from the real (Warzel, 2018).

Finally, false information is often spread because it touches on issues of deep concern—things people are quite passionate about, such as health care and politics. Often, there is deep-seated fear or uneasiness around the topic in question. Given this passion, it is tempting to quickly agree with and pass on information that confirms one's beliefs rather than fact-checking or pausing to verify its accuracy.

HAVING GOOD INFORMATION IS IMPORTANT

In preceding chapters, we have discussed the importance of access to information as a fundamental right protected by the First Amendment (Chapter 1). We have also talked about the importance of access for democracy (Chapters 2 and 4). To summarize, people need to have access to a wide range of perspectives in order to practice meaningful democracy. As the American Library Association (ALA) says,

> Intellectual freedom is the basis for our democratic system. We expect our people to be self-governors. But to do so responsibly, our citizenry must be well-informed. Libraries provide the ideas and information, in a variety of formats, to allow people to inform themselves. (ALA, 2007, para. 2)

In a democracy, people are considered "governors," meaning that the power of the government rests in the hands of the people. Politicians are voted in and out of office, based on their actions and positions. To make good decisions about whom to support and elect, people need good, reliable information. Intellectual freedom ensures that a wide variety of information is available, representing many different points of view. When many perspectives are available, people can become educated on a wide range of issues and viewpoints. People can access this range of perspectives, gain new information, and evaluate the various arguments on multiple sides of important issues.

As a result of their reading and reflection, people may decide to write to their representatives, petition for specific actions, protest other actions, or change their voting plans. In these ways, they can exercise their power and guide the direction of their democracy. Thus, intellectual freedom supports the democratic activity of citizens.

For example, an individual may become concerned about an increase in drug use in his or her state. To learn about this, the person may study the drugs involved, their origin, how they are distributed, the state's plans for catching and punishing criminals, rehabilitation and addiction recovery plans, and so on. The person may get this information from websites, books and other resources at the library, state agencies, politician platforms, and various other places.

Based on the information this person learns, he or she may change voting plans. Perhaps he or she will now vote for someone who is tougher on crime and vows to crack down on drug distribution. On the other hand, perhaps he or she plans to vote for someone who emphasizes rehabilitation and addiction treatment.

HOW THIS RELATES TO FALSE INFORMATION

The preceding discussion makes the need for a strong right to information access clear. It is essential for several reasons, including to help citizens in the democratic process. From this perspective, it may seem logical to think that libraries (of any type) should only have the most accurate, relevant, reliable, and meaningful information, designed to specifically be of assistance to voters who want to learn and be engaged.

However, limiting a library collection in this manner would be dangerous and shortsighted for at least two reasons. First, it is contrary to librarian ethics. Recall the Library Bill of Rights (ALA, 2006). Librarians have a responsibility to avoid excluding resources simply because of the viewpoint of the author or the librarians' own view of the work.

In the words of Asheim (1953), "To the selector, the important thing is to find reasons to keep the book. Given such a guiding principle, the selector looks for values, for strengths, for virtues which will over shadow [*sic*] minor objections" (para. 21). Librarians are trained to include good resources for their libraries. In contrast, says Asheim, censors look for reasons to exclude books.

Librarians cannot base their selection decisions on whether they personally approve of or agree with the content of the book (see Chapter 7 about collection development). On the contrary, librarians' personal opinions must be set aside to evaluate the materials neutrally, based on the collection development policy. This principle also applies to information that the librarian believes to be false.

Second, the definition of false information (or fake news) is unsettled. Some things may be called false today but determined to be true later or vice versa. Some works, especially sociological, political, or religious, may always have their truthfulness contested (or misunderstood). Just because something has been called fake news doesn't mean it can be automatically excluded. The phrase is used by different groups to mean different things.

For example, there were numerous debates about the structure and order of the universe throughout the past several centuries (including more recently, with the debate about whether Pluto should be considered a planet). You can imagine Galileo's view of the universe being called "fake news" back in his day. On a more serious note, the evidence in favor of human-caused climate change is overwhelming, yet some people remain skeptical (or dispute it even more strongly). Numerous books and websites purport to challenge the settled scientific view as false.

Simply put, fake news and misinformation cannot be automatically excluded from a library. That does not mean any and all sources of false information must be in every library. But it does mean the decision to exclude something cannot be taken lightly or easily.

HOW TO EVALUATE FALSE INFORMATION

Librarians should not feel powerless, however. We have tools, techniques, and resources to help us evaluate information. In fact, this is one of our essential professional strengths: reviewing and evaluating information.

One such tool is the library's collection development policy (as covered in Chapter 7, every library should have one). Most collection development policies include accuracy or truthfulness as a factor to consider when evaluating a potential purchase. Sometimes quality is another factor for consideration. Thus, items can be evaluated on these grounds. Many items that contain false information will not pass muster when assessed according to collection development guidelines.

To evaluate items with regard to accuracy or quality, we can look to reviews, which may address whether the item has been evaluated for accuracy by experts. We could also consider the classification of the item (e.g., is it supposed to be fiction or nonfiction?) and the publisher (what sorts of materials are they known for?).

In conjunction with the collection development policy, consider the library's budget. Does the library have sufficient resources to purchase items whose content may be false? Sometimes the answer to this question will be yes; sometimes no. Note, however, that the question was not about whether the library had sufficient resources to purchase an item that may be *controversial*. Fearing controversy should not be a sufficient reason to avoid purchasing an item; this is contrary to the ideals of intellectual freedom.

Even after using these tools, some items that could be considered false information may still become part of a library's collection. There are numerous reasons for this. It may be seen as necessary to have a well-rounded collection. To represent all views, some questionable material may have to be accepted into the collection. For example, your library may believe it needs to represent climate change skepticism within its collection to provide patrons with access to a variety of perspectives.

This brings up another tool that we can deploy to combat false information: information literacy. This means carefully evaluating the information we consume and thinking critically about it. As Agosto (2018) explains,

> Although school and academic librarians have been the most visible promoters of critical thinking and information evaluation as fundamental to their services, both concepts are core aspects of public, special, and government libraries services as well. . . . Librarians have both the opportunity and the responsibility to teach their communities how to determine whether the information they encounter online [and offline] is accurate, reliable, and worthy of being shared. (p. 2)

Patrons who are information literate, and confident in their information literacy, are less likely to fall prey to misinformation. Instead, they will be able to evaluate and recognize it for what it is.

In turn, information-literate individuals often help others with gaining access to information, creating a potential ripple effect of information literacy and overall reducing the effects of false information. This is one of the most important reasons to teach information literacy to one's patrons. False information will always be present—and will sometimes be in our libraries. Information literacy is the best tool to combat its presence.

SOME EXAMPLES OF HOW LIBRARIES HAVE DEALT WITH FALSE INFORMATION

Defending intellectual freedom, especially in relation to false information, can often be difficult, but the following incidents will provide further illumination as to how this can be done.

Vamos a Cuba

One intriguing case took place in Miami, Florida, in 2006. Parents challenged the inclusion of a children's book, *Vamos a Cuba*, in the school libraries because it did not accurately depict the oppression and difficulty of life in communist Cuba (Aguayo, 2006). The book, one in a series, portrayed a holiday in Cuba. Many Cuban expatriates living in Miami-Dade County saw the book as inaccurate and misleading. Despite recommendations from two committees to keep the book, the school board decided to remove *Vamos a Cuba* and the other twenty-three books in the series.

The American Civil Liberties Union (ACLU) filed suit, arguing that this was contradictory to the decision rendered in *Board of Education v. Pico* (1982). The Eleventh Circuit Court ruled that the book removal was acceptable, though many legal scholars and library experts disagree with the ruling (Fiore, 2011). The school board argued the books were removed due to inaccuracies, but many believed that the books were removed due to disagreement with their message—that is, the book did not condemn communism in Cuba. Under the guidelines established in the *Pico* case, removal due to inaccuracy would be acceptable, while removal because of partisan disapproval would not be.

From this case, librarians should remember that simple disagreement with a book is not enough of a reason to remove it or decline purchasing it. If the item contains inaccuracies, however, that is a sufficient reason. As this case shows, the line differentiating those two stances can be quite tricky to decipher. Librarians and others must be honest with themselves.

Children's Books about Slavery

Issues that were similarly complicated arose more recently, with the children's books *A Fine Dessert: Four Centuries, Four Families, One Delicious Treat* (by Emily Jenkins and Sophie Blackall) and *A Birthday Cake for George Washington* (by Ramin Ganeshram). Both of these books were criticized for their simplistic portrayal of slavery. For example, in *A Fine Dessert*, slaves are shown smiling while baking the dessert for the master's family and then hiding in the cupboard to lick the bowl clean. The main characters in *A Birthday Cake*, likewise, are slaves, depicted as resourceful, proud, and happy—though an author's note explains that the main character escaped slavery, leaving his daughter behind.

A Fine Dessert was published first and received positive reviews initially, before being scrutinized more carefully. The first author, Jenkins, eventually came to regret her book and its insensitive portrayal of slavery (Smith, 2016). When *A Birthday Cake* was released, it faced criticism almost immediately and the publisher soon pulled the book (Peralta, 2016).

Libraries faced uncertainty with these books: Should they be purchased? If they were purchased, then subject to criticism and suspended publication, should they be withdrawn? If left on the shelves, should a caution or explanatory note be offered?

Libraries have answered these questions differently, depending on their community, their collection development policy, and the stance of their director or board. Few libraries own either book, as a simple search on WorldCat reveals. Often the books, if purchased, were withdrawn from the library collection due to perceived inaccuracies. Librarians generally hesitate to put "warnings" on books, as this can be seen as a form of label (which the ALA opposes) or as a way to prejudice the reader against a book. While the ALA did not issue formal guidance regarding these books, the National Coalition Against Censorship (NCAC) did oppose withdrawing the books.

The Seventies

One final example is worth considering. In their research into book challenges in public libraries and schools, Peterson, Oltmann, and Knox (2017) uncovered a challenge to a nonfiction book in an Alabaman public library. One patron complained that a book, *The Seventies: The Great Shift in American Culture, Society, and Politics* (by Bruce Shulman), falsely depicted the rock band Lynyrd Skynyrd as racist.

After reviewing the title, the director recommended retaining the book but adding additional resources to provide another perspective. This is often the most appropriate way to deal with content that may be perceived to have some bias. Supplementing the collection with additional viewpoints provides more information so that patrons can develop their own informed views. This also aids information literacy and strengthens the library's collection.

CONCLUSION

In this chapter, we have reviewed some of the definitions and components of false information (also known as "fake news"). We have demonstrated that false information can be a particular concern for libraries, especially from an intellectual freedom perspective. We cannot simply reject all information that people claim is false, as that would likely decimate sections of our libraries, particularly those that contain controversial or contentious topics. Instead, we must follow our collection development policies and carefully maintain balanced collections. We must also promote information literacy within our libraries, teaching and guiding patrons to thoughtfully evaluate their information sources.

Let's reconsider the book *Arming America*, mentioned at the beginning of the chapter. As described previously, it was challenged for fabrications and problems with citations, after many academic and public libraries had purchased it. When these problems came to light, libraries faced a dilemma concerning whether they should keep the book.

At the time of the controversy, many libraries decided to exclude the book from their collections because the falsehoods in it were clearly countered by evidence. Today, few (if any) still retain copies.

This was a book that was proven to have fabrications and outright lies. It thus did not meet collection development policies that included accuracy as one consideration for inclusion. Because it did not meet collection development policies, libraries were justified in removing it from their collections.

REFERENCES

Agosto, D. E. (Ed.). (2018). *Information Literacy and libraries in the age of fake news*. Santa Barbara, CA: Libraries Unlimited.

Aguayo, T. (2006). Miami-Dade school board bans Cuba book. *New York Times*. Retrieved from https://www.nytimes.com/2006/06/16/education/16cuba.html.

American Library Association. (2006). Library bill of rights. Retrieved from http://www.ala.org/advocacy/intfreedom/librarybill. Document ID: 669fd6a3-8939-3e54-7577-996a0a3f8952.

American Library Association. (2007). Intellectual freedom and censorship Q&A. Retrieved from http://www.ala.org/advocacy/intfreedom/censorship/faq. Document ID: e8ae9ed7-a469-f0d4-adf0-f2770d2ca8e8.

Asheim, L. E. (1953). Not censorship, but selection. *Wilson Library Bulletin, 28,* 63–67. Retrieved from http://www.ala.org/advocacy/intfreedom/NotCensorshipButSelection

Board of Education, Island Trees Union Free School District No. 26 v. Pico, 457 U.S. 853 (1982).

Cooke, N. A. (2018). Critical literacy as an approach to combating cultural misinformation/disinformation on the internet. In D. E. Agosto (Ed.), *Information Literacy and libraries in the age of fake news* (pp. 36–51). Santa Barbara, CA: Libraries Unlimited.

Fiore, K. (2011). ACLU v. Miami-Dade County School Board: Reading *Pico* imprecisely, writing undue restrictions on public school library books, and adding to the collection of students' First Amendment right violations. *Villanova Law Review, 56*(1), 97–128.

Froehlich, T. J. (2017). A not-so-brief account of current information ethics: The ethics of ignorance, missing information, misinformation, disinformation, and other forms of deception or incompetence. *BID: Biblioteconomia i documentacio, 39.* Retrieved from http://bid.ub.edu/en/39/froehlich.htm

McLemee, S. (2010). Amazing disgrace. Inside Higher Ed. Retrieved from https://www.insidehighered.com/views/2010/05/19/amazing-disgrace

Peralta, E. (2016). Amid controversy, Scholastic pulls picture book about Washington's slave. NPR. Retrieved from https://www.npr.org/sections/thetwo-way/2016/01/18/463488364/amid-controversy-scholastic-pulls-picture-book-about-washingtons-slave

Peterson, C., Oltmann, S. M., & Knox, E.J.M. (2017). The inconsistent work of web filters: Mapping information access in Alabama public schools and libraries. *International Journal of Communication, 11.* Retrieved from https://ijoc.org/index.php/ijoc/article/view/6944

Smith, V. (2016). Smiling slaves in a post-A Fine Dessert world. Kirkus Reviews. Retrieved from https://www.kirkusreviews.com/features/smiling-slaves-post-fine-dessert-world/

Vosoughi, S., Roy, D., & Aral, S. (2018). The spread of true and false news online. *Science, 359*(6380), 1146–1151. Retrieved from http://science.sciencemag.org/content/359/6380/1146

Warzel, C. (2018). He predicted the 2016 fake news crisis. Now he's worried about an information apocalypse. BuzzFeed News. Retrieved from https://www.buzzfeednews.com/article/charliewarzel/the-terrifying-future-of-fake-news

Wood, M. (2018). One problem with fake news? It really, really works. NPR Marketplace. Retrieved from https://www.marketplace.org/2018/08/24/tech/one-problem-fake-news-it-really-really-works

TWELVE

Law Enforcement and Intellectual Freedom

Local law enforcement means your local police department, campus security, county sheriff, and so on—whoever is responsible for keeping the peace and enforcing order in your community (and remember, community means the groups of patrons that your library serves). Many libraries are unsure about the sort of relationship they should have with their local law enforcement.

In general, the relationship should be courteous and respectful; remember that they are also professionals like librarians are. At times, local law enforcement may be helpful to your library (e.g., when a patron is violating the law).

However, at other times, there may be sometimes tension in the relationship, particularly when law enforcement is seeking information about patrons. This can be complicated and tricky to navigate because of the library profession's emphasis on patron privacy.

Imagine that there has been a recent spate of arson in the community. No one has gotten hurt so far, but several buildings have been damaged; there is considerable concern in the community that these crimes will escalate. The police come to the library and ask who has checked out certain books that discuss fires similar to the ones they are investigating. What should your library do? How should the library respond to this request?

In the following sections, we will discuss different types of requests from law enforcement and the best ways to respond to them. Throughout this chapter, you will see the importance of having an attorney for your library. Often, if your library has a parent organization (e.g., the university for an academic library), legal counsel is available in that way. Regardless of the approach, however, it is wise to have legal advice available for when your library needs it.

POSITIVE RELATIONSHIPS WITH LAW ENFORCEMENT

First, we should note that it is an excellent idea to develop a positive relationship between local law enforcement and your library. There may be unfortunate times that your library needs to rely on a positive relationship with local law enforcement. Perhaps a patron is being unruly, unreasonable, or simply not following library policy. Perhaps a dangerous situation has occurred.

Once, when I was interviewing a library director about intellectual freedom policies, he had to cut our meeting short. A man with a gun had entered the library and was intimidating some patrons. The security guard on duty in the library was unsure whether to call the police. The director went to assess the situation and quickly determined that a police presence would help stabilize the situation, so they were called to the scene. This is an example of a time when a positive relationship with the local law enforcement was useful.

Another story comes from Massachusetts, where library staff called police because they believed patrons were engaging in a drug deal in the restroom. Police arrived and did, in fact, catch two men with drugs and paraphernalia; they were subsequently arrested and charged (Lamont, 2018). If a library has developed good relationships with local law enforcement, these sorts of situations can go more smoothly.

Regardless of the reason, your library will want to be able to call upon law enforcement with confidence. Because these sorts of problems can occur unexpectedly or escalate rapidly, it's a good idea to keep contact information for law enforcement near the main desks and offices. Sometimes local law enforcement officers will share their personal contact information, and this, also, should be shared as appropriate.

To foster positive relationships with law enforcement officials, there are a few steps your library can take. First, be respectful and thoughtful of the officials' time. Do not call them out unnecessarily or waste their time once they are in the library. Second, be gracious and thank them for their assistance. Third, to the extent possible, cooperate with their requests for assistance. This is a complicated area and is the focus of the rest of the chapter.

REQUESTS FROM LAW ENFORCEMENT

Requests from law enforcement can take many forms, which we will discuss here. First, law enforcement officials may simply ask for information pertaining to a case. Perhaps they want to know if a certain individual is or was in the library, who checked out certain materials, or information about computer usage. This can be called a "request for information" and does not have any legal status, as it is a simple appeal.

A second type of request from law enforcement officials is called a *warrant*. Typically, warrants are issued by judges or other legal officials. They grant permission to law enforcement officials to arrest a suspect, search premises, and conduct other activities for the administration of the law; different types of warrants are needed for each activity. A search warrant must describe the items that are to be looked for in sufficient detail. Usually the items are related to the commission of a crime. There must be probable cause to issue a search warrant (meaning a strong likelihood that the items sought exist and are in the location to be searched).

In general, search warrants must be shown when the search begins. Law enforcement officials may have a search warrant for library information such as computer usage logs or circulation records. Warrants are immediately executable, which means that law enforcement does not have to let library staff consult a lawyer before collecting the information.

Another type of request is a *subpoena*, which is a court-ordered command to do something, such as produce documents or appear in court. These are typically created by a court clerk, a notary public, or a justice of the peace. People who receive a subpoena must comply or face civil or criminal penalties (e.g., fines or jail time); ignoring a subpoena is often considered contempt of court. Though these are often not delivered by law enforcement officials, they are part of the legal system, so they will be considered here. Subpoenas may be issued for similar information as warrants, to mandate bringing certain library records to the courtroom.

In addition to warrants and subpoenas, some law enforcement agencies will execute an *open records request* for information. Some libraries (particularly school libraries, public libraries, and academic libraries at public universities) are covered under laws that make government records available to the public. These laws are known as open records laws, freedom of information laws, or sunshine laws. The goal is to make government information available to the general public so the public can hold government agencies accountable, but the records requests can be used for many other purposes, including law enforcement. When used by law enforcement, open records requests must be processed and answered the same as any other request.

A final type of request that few libraries will receive—but is still important to know about—is a *National Security Letter.* This most often originates from the Federal Bureau of Investigation (FBI) and sometimes from other federal government agencies, too. It focuses on investigations related to national security. Unlike warrants, National Security Letters do not need approval from a judge and do not need to invoke probable cause (only "reasonable cause," a lower legal standard).

Furthermore, when an institution receives a National Security Letter, the institution cannot disclose its receipt to anyone other than a lawyer (in particular, it cannot be disclosed to the subject of the investigation). While libraries have rarely been the target of National Security Letters, it has occasionally happened (see American Library Association [ALA], 2009).

It is important to note that, once one receives a warrant, subpoena, or National Security Letter, it is illegal to destroy any records that are implicated by these documents. Instead, the records must be protected and maintained and then turned over as indicated.

FIRST STEPS IN RESPONDING TO LAW ENFORCEMENT

Responses to law enforcement will depend on what type of request they are making, the type of information they are seeking, and the relevant laws in your state. However, before we get to those specific responses, there are some general guidelines that are applicable across the board.

The first step is to remain calm and courteous. Typically, the law enforcement official will ask to speak to a supervisor and hand over the warrant or the relevant documents. If the official just addresses whoever is at the front desk, however, it is appropriate to ask for a supervisor or the director immediately. People at an administrative level should have more training and understanding of these situations (see later for information about training). In addition, everyone involved should remain courteous. Remember that the law enforcement officials are just performing their job duties.

Next, ask for any supporting documentation. If there are not any accompanying documents, then you are faced with a simple request by law enforcement officials (as opposed to a legal order to produce information or records). You should be able to view warrants, subpoenas, and National Security Letters. Read the documents carefully to see what is covered; you should only allow access to data that are explicitly included in the documentation. Though some law enforcement officials may try to persuade you otherwise, you do not (and should not) have to provide access to anything else. If possible, have an attorney review the documents.

Third, the person in charge, whoever is reviewing and responding to the documents, will have to decide whether to acquiesce to the order or challenge it. (Note that warrants are, as stated previously, immediately executable, so they can't be challenged before they are acted upon.) If the decision is to accept the order, then the next step is to produce the records or the information that is sought. If the decision is to challenge the order, then an attorney will almost certainly need to be consulted to determine the next steps.

DECIDING HOW TO RESPOND

How should you respond to the various types of requests and orders? First, determine whether it is a simple request or a legally backed request (supported by a warrant, subpoena, open records request, or National Security Letter). If this is a simple request, then you do not need to turn over any records or information. You can politely decline to share information.

In most states, in fact, library records are considered confidential information and may not be shared *without* a court order or records request. You should be familiar with the laws of your state in this regard; many law enforcement officials will not know the specifics of library record policies, so it is incumbent on librarians to know this information. Your state library association should be able to supply this information if needed.

However, if there is supporting documentation, such as a warrant, a subpoena, an open records request, or a National Security Letter, then you will need to determine how to respond. Most of the time, most libraries will agree to provide the requested information. This may be information about who checked out particular items, who was in the library at certain times (which could be verifiable through security footage), usage statistics for certain computers, and so on—there is actually quite a bit of data that are generated by ordinary library usage. Many times, law enforcement is seeking information for legitimate purposes to determine who committed a crime.

There are a few questions you can ask as you consider how to respond. First, consider whether the information actually exists. Let's imagine that law enforcement officials want to determine if someone was in the library at a certain time. They could demand footage from a security camera. If law enforcement seeks security footage but there are no security cameras, then you simply can't fulfill the request.

This is an important question to consider when deciding what patron-related information to collect; if you don't collect it, it can't be turned over to law enforcement. As a result of this line of thought, many libraries do not maintain records of computer usage (e.g., who signed onto computers, which sites they visited, what they did). The information is simply cleared out every time someone logs out.

Second, is this the best way—the only way—to get the information that law enforcement is seeking? In the example about a patron's location, law enforcement might ask librarians if someone was present. Instead, law enforcement could possibly use traffic cameras to pinpoint a car's location in/near the library parking lot, without using library data.

A third question to consider has to do with the breadth of the information sought. Is the information requested the minimum amount needed to satisfy law enforcement's need? Let's consider the example cited earlier. Perhaps library security camera footage *is* the best way to get the information that law enforcement needs, but they likely only need information for a short window of time. This question can avoid fishing expeditions, giving away more patron information than is really needed by law enforcement.

Finally, as mentioned earlier, consider asking the library's attorney to weigh in. Even small libraries should have an attorney on retainer, someone who is willing to consider legal issues on behalf of the library. An attorney will likely be needed rarely, but in those cases where a professional legal opinion is needed, it is invaluable. Again, state library associations should be able to help libraries find attorneys who are willing to assist.

SOME EXAMPLES TO CONSIDER

Sometimes these issues are easier to understand in the context of specific examples. Following are a few situations in which law enforcement has interacted with library staff and sought library information.

A Missing Preteen Girl

An emotional case occurred in a public library in Vermont in 2008, when a twelve-year-old girl went missing. Police had a tip that she frequently used the library computers, and they wanted to take the computers in question. The library staff requested a warrant first, which was legally correct and in line with professional ethics, which support protecting patron information as much as possible.

After a heated confrontation, the law enforcement officials left, secured a warrant within eight hours, and came back to take the computers (Associated Press, 2008). The girl, sadly, was later found dead, abducted and killed by her uncle. In this case, the library staff were abiding by professional ethics, protecting the privacy of their patrons. Because the library director requested a warrant, she ensured that the law enforcement officers were not seeking the computers for a frivolous reason and were limited in what they could search for.

Cameras in the Public Library?

Recently, public libraries in Lebanon, New Hampshire, debated whether to install security cameras. Concern developed because of an alleged sexual assault that occurred several months earlier in the library. After this incident, library staff and trustees formed a committee to study whether the two libraries should install security cameras.

The committee, after reviewing relevant evidence and information, decided to forego camera installation. They determined that cameras were not really a crime prevention tool; while cameras might help solve thefts, the libraries dealt with few thefts. When they balanced these issues with concerns about patron privacy and comfort, they decided that cameras would not be beneficial for the libraries (Camerato, 2017).

National Security Letter in Connecticut

In 2005, a library in Connecticut received a National Security Letter, requesting information about which patrons had used the computers during a specific period a year earlier. Any patron who had used the computers during that time period could be under suspicion but would never know, because of the "gag order" effect of the National Security Letter—no one, other than an attorney, can be told of the receipt of such a letter.

The library was part of a consortium, so the director told the consortium board members about the National Security Letter (even though it was unclear if he was legally allowed to do so). The board members decided to challenge the constitutionality of the National Security Letter. The case became known as *Doe v. Gonzales* and then *Doe v. Ashcroft*. (The board members filed the lawsuit as John and Jane Does to protect their identities. If they had not done so, they could have been jailed for revealing they received a National Security Letter.)

After a year of legal maneuvering—during which the Patriot Act's expanded authority for the use of National Security Letters was reapproved—the government dropped the case. The board members were finally allowed to speak about the case. They revealed they had challenged the National Security Letter because they felt the breadth and the gag order were unconstitutional. It did not seem right to them that the government could have such sweeping powers (Cowan, 2006). To date, the courts have not yet ruled on the constitutionality of the gag orders associated with National Security Letters.

CONCLUSION

In the years since the Connecticut case, it remains unclear how many libraries have received National Security Letters because they continue to have gag orders attached to them. It is known that potential and actual terrorists have used library resources—for example, some of the 9/11 terrorists used public library computers in Florida (Rosenbaum, 2001). This means that it is likely that some libraries have been, and will continue to be, institutions of interest to the FBI and other law enforcement agencies.

Interestingly, we know that two of the 9/11 terrorists used public library computers in Florida because a librarian recognized their names (after their crimes) and called the FBI to report their activities in the library. This actually violated both Florida law and professional ethics, though many at the time felt that the librarian had a duty to share the information with law enforcement. It remains a complex example of professional ethics intersecting with a horrific real-life situation.

Let's return to the scenario described at the beginning of the chapter: a spate of arson in the community leads local law enforcement to ask for library records pertaining to books with a similar kind of fire. What should a library do in this situation?

The first step is to determine what type of request law enforcement is making and then respond accordingly. Even though the library staff may want to help law enforcement solve these cases, they should follow professional ethics and ask law enforcement for a warrant for this information. That will ensure that law enforcement does not fall into a habit of seeking information without proper justification.

Once a warrant is signed, the information sought can be turned over (if it exists). Many libraries, however, do not keep long-term circulation records, so the information the police seek may not exist. Regardless, remember to practice professionalism and respect for all people involved.

REFERENCES

American Library Association. (2009). ALA and national security letters. Retrieved from http://www.ala.org/news/mediapresscenter/presscenter/onlinemessagebook/nationalsecurityletters_tp. Document ID: 31352bd5-6524-f744-11c6-8593b852761f.

Associated Press. (2008). Girl's case had library, cops in privacy standoff. NBCNews.com. Retrieved from http://www.nbcnews.com/id/25751801/ns/us_news-security/t/girls-case-had-library-cops-privacy-standoff/#.W_HTPOhKiU1

Camerato, T. (2017). No cameras for Lebanon libraries. *Valley News.* Retrieved from https://www.vnews.com/Lebanon-Libraries-to-Forgo-Cameras-14296725

Cowan, A.L. (2006). Four librarians finally break silence in records case. *New York Times.* Retrieved from https://www.nytimes.com/2006/05/31/nyregion/31library.html?_r=0

Lamont, R. (2018). Police: Men made drug deal in library bathroom. *Gloucester Daily Times.* Retrieved from https://www.gloucestertimes.com/news/local_news/police-men-made-drug-deal-in-library-bathroom/article_08c3f239-77b8-5ec0-9aaf-a9c0c75b31d6.html

Rosenbaum, D.E. (2001). A nation challenged: Questions of confidentiality; competing principles leave some professionals debating responsibility to government. *New York Times.* Retrieved from https://www.nytimes.com/2001/11/23/us/nation-challenged-questions-confidentiality-competing-principles-leave-some.html

THIRTEEN

Copyright Issues

Copyright may seem like a very broad issue that is not specific to libraries or to intellectual freedom. In many ways this statement is correct—copyright *is* incredibly broad, and many of the challenges associated with copyright law and usage are not specific to libraries.

Yet, within libraries, copyright is an important issue. It governs and regulates much of the daily activities of libraries, even if we don't necessarily think of these as related to copyright. In addition, copyright law places restrictions on what librarians and patrons can do with items that are copyrighted (which would include most items in most libraries).

Here is an example of how copyright may affect libraries. A school librarian was asked by a teacher to find an e-book version of *Frankenstein* by Mary Shelley so that the teacher could share the e-book with all of her students (over 150 students across all her classes). The librarian had no funds for this request but wanted to find something that was copyright compliant. She wasn't sure how to determine whether this sort of usage would be permissible within the copyright law.

Where should the librarian in this scenario turn? How can she determine if the teacher's request would be copyright compliant? How can the librarian find an e-book that meets the teacher's needs?

In this chapter, we will review the basic foundations of copyright law, the three special provisions that relate to libraries, and other issues and perspectives on copyright. This will provide you with the information needed to make legally appropriate decisions on copyright.

OVERVIEW OF COPYRIGHT LAW AND PURPOSE

In the United States, copyright is enshrined in the Constitution.[1] In Article I, the Constitution states that the U.S. Congress shall have the power "to promote the Progress of Science and useful Arts, by securing for limited Times to Authors and Inventors[2] the exclusive Right to their respective Writings and Discoveries" (Article I, Sec. 8, Clause 8). This clause means that writers and other creators have certain rights when it comes to the things they've created. Let's explore this in more detail.

The idea behind copyright protection is simple: people have labored to produce something (e.g., a novel, play, or video), and they deserve to benefit from their efforts. Copyright law enables the creator to own several rights related to the work they've created and to reap the rewards from that work—including monetary rewards. For example, if you've written a best-selling novel, you deserve to profit from the time and energy you put into it. Copyright law is the mechanism we have to ensure that happens.

Beyond profit, there is another reason to have copyright law: attribution. If that best-selling novel did not have your name on it—did not have any name on it—that might lower your motivation to write again or at all.

Imagine a world where no one who created anything was given credit. Surely, in this world, fewer people would be motivated to create things such as music, art, and poetry. Society as a whole would be worse off with less art. This is one of the arguments in favor of copyright protection.

What Is Covered by Copyright Law?

Works covered by copyright include literary works, musical works, dramatic works, pantomimes and choreography, pictorial, graphic, and sculptural works, motion pictures and other audiovisual works, sound recordings, and architectural works (Copyright law, 1976, section 102).

The law explicitly notes that copyright protection does not "extend to any idea, procedure, process, system, method of operation, concept, principle, or discovery" (Copyright law, 1976, section 102, para. b). If you think about it, this makes sense. Only tangible works can be copyrighted. Things like ideas are intangible and cannot be fixed in a particular format. Furthermore, many ideas are used again and again (think of "love songs" as an example); it's the particular form and shape that an idea takes (e.g., a particular song, novel, or poem) that can be copyrighted.

When a creation or work is copyrighted, there are actual several distinct rights involved. One right, as you might expect, is the right to reproduce (or copy) the work. A second right is to distribute the copies through sales, rentals, lending, or ownership transfer. Copyright owners can also prepare derivative works (e.g., a screenplay drawn from a novel) based on the copyrighted work. Owners also have the right to perform or display the work publicly. All of these things you can do with or to a work are protected by copyright law.

These rights take effect immediately when something is copyrighted. To copyright something you have created (e.g., a novel), the main criterion is that it be "fixed in a tangible medium." In other words, it needs to be written or recorded in some way that is fairly immutable. Jotting down song lyrics in a notebook would count. Writing a poem on a dry-erase board would probably not be copyrightable because it would not be fixed—it could easily be erased or changed. However, recording yourself in a video or audio would create a copyrightable work.

Once something is fixed in a tangible medium, it is automatically granted copyright in the United States. That's actually all you have to do. However, to make your copyright claim more substantial and easier to prove, you should register your work with the Copyright Office. Details of how to do so can be found on their website (https://www.copyright.gov/).

When an item is protected by copyright, permission must be sought to use it, perform it, copy it, and so on. To do so, you must contact the copyright holder (usually the creator) and get permission in writing. Often there is a fee to use the work. For example, when a theater troupe performs a play, they generally have paid a royalty fee to the playwright for performance rights to perform the copyrighted work.

This demonstrates how copyright protects creators' rights to profit and benefit from their work. Without such fees, anyone could perform the play without giving proper attribution (or payment) to the playwright. If no playwrights received attribution, that would greatly reduce the incentive to write plays, and society as a whole would suffer a decrease in art and creative works.

Length of Copyright Protection

Copyright on most things (produced in 1978 or later) lasts for the life of the author/creator plus seventy years. For works created prior to 1978, the length of copyright varies considerably. In addition, works created "for hire" (meaning created for your employer and owned by your employer) are copyrighted for up to 120 years from the year of their creation. (Again, the Copyright Office should be consulted for details about the length of copyright protection, especially for items created prior to 1978.) The Copyright Office argues that this length of time is necessary for creators to fully benefit from their efforts to create works.

When the copyright protections for a particular work expire, the work becomes part of the public domain. This means that it is no longer protected by copyright law; anyone can now copy, distribute, reproduce, display, or perform it. Generally, most works created prior to 1923 are in the public domain because their copyright protection has expired (although certain performances or productions of pre-1923 works may be copyrighted).

THREE IMPORTANT LIMITATIONS ON COPYRIGHT PROTECTIONS

As the preceding discussion explains, copyright law can provide vast protections for an enormous breadth of works. However, copyright law does have some limitations. Three of them are particularly important and relevant for libraries.

First Sale Doctrine

According to the first sale doctrine of U.S. copyright law, the copyright holder has the right to benefit from the first sale of the copyrighted work. After that, whoever has purchased that particular copy has the right to do whatever they want with it.

So, when you buy a book of poetry, the poet benefits from that sale. Then, you own that particular book and you can lend it, sell it, copy poems from it, and so on. You are able to use your copy of the work however you see fit.

The importance of this to libraries would be hard to overstate. Libraries of all kinds purchase creative content continually, and (some of) the proceeds of those purchases go to the creators of those works. Then libraries may use those works as they want to—namely, lending them out to their patrons. Without the first sale doctrine, the central activity of most libraries would be impossible. Libraries would not be able to lend items.

Reproduction for Libraries and Archives

In addition to the first sale doctrine, the law allows libraries and archives, under certain conditions, to make reproductions of some of the content they own (often called the "Section 108 exception"). The reproduction must be made with no anticipation of "direct or indirect commercial advantage" because that would infringe upon the copyright holder's rights.

Generally, the library or archive can only create one reproduction of a given work. It must be open to the general public or to people using the specialized research area. Finally, you have to include a copyright notice (or a note that the work may be protected under copyright law).

Reasons to use this exception include patron requests for articles or short excerpts. Libraries and archives may also use this exception to make up to three archival reproductions of unpublished works, as long as they are not published or made available digitally outside the premises. In some cases, this can also cover making a copy of a rare or damaged item.

This exception facilitates interlibrary loan (ILL) and cooperation among libraries, but it should not be abused. It's important to note that reproduction in these cases should be isolated and relatively rare. Such reproduction should not substitute for a subscription to a journal, for example; if your library uses this exception to obtain numerous ILL copies of articles from a particular journal, it should consider subscribing to that journal.

Fair Use Principle

The third exception to copyright law that is important for libraries (and many other types of organizations) is called the "fair use doctrine." Technically, this is not an *exception* to copyright; it is only considered a "legal defense." This means if you share or use a copyrighted work, you may be able to claim fair use justifiably.

If your use of a copyrighted work is "fair use," it means you do not need to get permission from the copyright holder or pay a fee to use the work. Thus, it is tempting to interpret fair use broadly and claim that whatever you're doing should be considered fair use.

Before you do so, however, you must consider the four factors that determine whether a use of a copyrighted work is considered fair use. The four factors are the purpose and character of the use, the nature of the copyrighted work, the amount and substantiality of the portion used, and the effect on the potential market. Let's take each of these in turn.

When considering the purpose and character of the use, such things as criticism, comment, news reporting, education, scholarship, or research are more likely to be considered fair use. Using the copyrighted work for nonprofit purposes instead of commercial purposes is more likely to be considered fair use, though this is not a hard rule. In addition, educational purposes are likely to considered fair use. Finally, works that are transformational in nature may be fair use.

Next, you need to consider the nature of the copyrighted work. If the copyrighted work is published or factual/nonfiction, use of it may be more likely to be considered fair use. If the work is unpublished, fiction, and/or highly creative, use of it is probably less likely to be considered fair use.

The third factor of fair use is the amount and substantiality of the copyrighted work that is used. When using the whole work, a large portion of it, or a portion that is central to the work, this use is less likely to be considered fair use. However, if you use a small quantity and/or a portion that is not central, that may be considered fair use. Also, if the amount you use seems to serve an educational purpose, that indicates it may be fair use as well.

Finally, consider the effect on the potential market for the copyrighted work. First, if you lawfully own or acquire the item and your use of it will have little or no effect on the potential market for selling the copyrighted item, that is probably fair use. If your use could replace the sale of a copyrighted work, if it negatively affects the market for the work, if you made numerous copies, or if affordable permission was available, then your use would probably not be considered fair use. If you make a copyrighted work available on the internet, this will likely not be fair use either.

It's important to consider all four factors together when determining whether a particular use is fair use. No single factor is more important than the other, and no single factor outweighs the other.

For example, some people see that educational purposes tend to be considered fair use, so in their minds, they weigh that heavily and don't pay attention to the other three factors. This can happen often in schools and school libraries. However, this is not an appropriate interpretation of the fair use principle. If you are using a work for educational purposes, but it is a highly creative work, you are using a substantial portion of it, or you made multiple copies of it, then it may not be fair use.

Perhaps the most important thing to remember about fair use is that there are not cut-and-dried rules about what is or is not considered fair use. This is also the most confusing and frustrating thing about fair use. It has the potential to save users' time and money, but this principle must be deployed cautiously. Each time you want to use a copyrighted work, you need to consider all four factors equally.

LIBRARIES AND COPYRIGHT

Copyright is an important issue for libraries of all types for several reasons. As discussed previously, some of the key principles of copyright law (e.g., the first sale doctrine and the clause for libraries' and archives' reproduction) enable much of the day-to-day activities of libraries. Without these clauses, the legality of lending items and sharing ILL items would be in jeopardy.

Similarly, the fair use principle is exceptionally important for libraries. Many patrons come into libraries to gain access to information that they wish to keep; they may want to copy part of a book, for example. To determine whether this is legally allowable, libraries and patrons alike can deploy the fair use principle (using the four factors described earlier).

However, many patrons do not know about the fair use principle, many would not understand how to apply it, and some might not care about whether their use was within fair use. This can put libraries in a quandary, as your institution could be inadvertently facilitating someone violating copyright.

If a patron wanted to copy or scan a few poems from a book for personal (noncommercial) use, that would likely be fair use and would not need prior permission from the copyright holder. In contrast, if the patron wanted to copy every poem in the book or wanted to use these poems for business reasons, that use would probably no longer be fair use and would instead require permission from the copyright holder.

To protect against potential liability from this sort of issue, libraries should always ensure that they have a copyright warning near copy machines and scanners. Having this information prominently displayed will protect the library from liability from copyright infringement due to patron action. The Copyright and Fair Use office of the Stanford University Libraries notes that, generally, libraries will not be liable "based upon a library patron's unsupervised use of reproducing equipment located on its premises, provided that the copying equipment displays a notice that the making of a copy may be subject to the copyright law" (2018, para. 1). The copyright notice should include the following text:

> The copyright law of the United States (Title 17, United States Code) governs the making of photocopies or other reproductions of copyrighted material. Under certain conditions specified in the law, libraries and archives are authorized to furnish a photocopy or other reproduction. One of these specified conditions is that the photocopy or reproduction is not to be "used for any purpose other than private study, scholarship, or research." If a user makes a request for, or later uses, a photocopy or reproduction for purposes in excess of "fair use," that user may be liable for copyright infringement. This institution reserves the right to refuse to accept a copying order if, in its judgment, fulfillment of the order would involve violation of copyright law.

What should a librarian do if he or she suspects a patron is violating copyright? There are numerous anecdotes of librarians who discover patrons photocopying an entire book, for example. This would be a clear violation of fair use principles (because of the substantiality of the use and the potential impact on future sales).

In such a scenario, the librarian should speak to the patron. Let the patron know about the fair use principles and that his or her actions are violating copyright law. Suggest alternatives: Can they check the book out? Can they make do with a smaller portion of the book (maybe a few chapters)? Is a cheap copy available for sale online? Once you have notified the patron that he or she is violating copyright law, that individual must make a decision about whether to continue doing so. That decision is out of the hands of the librarian—and is not the librarian's legal responsibility.

Challenges with copyright often arise in school and academic libraries, where librarians are presumed to be copyright experts. In these institutions, there is often much copying and borrowing of work that go on. Teachers, for example, may want to copy worksheets out of a book or ensure that all students have access to a particular piece of writing. They may turn to the local librarian for advice about what is legally allowed (i.e., what is considered fair use).

For this reason, librarians should be familiar with copyright issues—especially school and academic librarians. Beyond familiarity, librarians may wish to take additional training to learn more about copyright issues and how to apply fair use principles. There are also many helpful resources online that can provide guidance. Teachers and others may be disappointed to learn the limitations of fair use, but it is better to stay in legal compliance.

The issues can be more complex, especially when dealing with video, audio, or online resources. The copyright law has not been updated for decades, so it is sometimes complicated to interpret it in relation to these newer forms.

Copyright is not only a library issue but also an intellectual freedom issue. Owners who are excessively protective of their copyrighted work are essentially preventing others from accessing and using it; an argument can also be made that they are inhibiting the creation of new works (since every creative work builds on what came before, in some way).

Copyright owners can charge fees for others to use their work (called "permission fees"). When these fees are high, it creates a differentiated sort of access: those with fewer resources will be unable to use the work.

PROBLEMS AND CHALLENGES WITH COPYRIGHT

As the preceding sections have made clear, copyright can be an incredibly complex area of law. There are a number of problem areas that scholars and advocates have identified over the years.

If the Use Is Not Fair Use

If you want to use a copyrighted work and your use doesn't fall under the fair use principle, you have to seek permission from the copyright holder. There are at least two potential issues that arise. First, it may be impossible to locate the copyright holder. Perhaps the original author or creator has died and the current ownership is unclear, or perhaps you know the copyright holder, but there are no further contact details available. Under these conditions, we call the work an "orphan work."

You must conduct a thorough and comprehensive search for the copyright holder before determining something is an orphan work. As the Copyright Office notes, "For good faith users, orphan works are a frustration, a liability risk, and a major cause of gridlock in the digital marketplace" (Copyright Office, 2015, p. 35). Be cautious in determining something is an orphaned work. Often, libraries and archives decide to not digitize orphaned works because they do not want to be liable later for copyright damages.

A different scenario can arise when the copyright holder is known and contact information is available. In these cases, the permission fee (to use the copyrighted work) is determined by the copyright holder. Generally the fee is not high, but in some cases, it can be exorbitant. This is more likely to be true when the copyright is held by a commercial entity.

Length of Copyright

One of the often-noted challenges has to do with the *length* of copyright. When the law was first written, copyright protection lasted fourteen years, with an option to renew for another fourteen years. Over time, Congress has extended copyright protection, which now lasts for the life of the author plus seventy years (as noted earlier, this can vary depending on the publication year of the work in question).

The length of copyright was extended to protect the rights of creators, primarily the right to profit from one's work. However, advocates for change remind us that one of the premises of copyright is to help society improve and inspire new creative works by allowing access to current creative works. The current law, by protecting copyright so long, hinders this sort of creative process. As a result, some people advocate for a change to this aspect of the law.

When Fair Use Is Too Vague

Some critics of copyright law claim that the fair use principle is too restrictive and too vague to be helpful. They argue that many more uses of copyrighted works, especially for educational or noncommercial reasons, should be allowed without having to go through contortions to figure out if that use is covered by our current principle of fair use. A classic example is the use of a popular song as background music in a video that someone uploads. Often this is claimed (by those who own the copyright) to be an infringement, and the original poster is forced to take the video down or face potential legal action.

Because it is hard to determine when use of a copyrighted work is fair use, many libraries and users err on the side of caution. In many academic libraries, for example, librarians have developed guidelines for faculty regarding fair use. The 10 percent rule seems common: if you are using less than 10 percent of a book, then it is considered fair use, and you do not need to get copyright permission.

This rule was developed from an abundance of caution—the law does not actually give a specific percentage like this. It is easier to state this rule than explain the fair use principles to faculty members who probably don't care about the details of copyright. It's worth realizing, however, that this is probably stricter than the fair use principles would suggest.

Licensing and Access

One significant way that copyright impacts libraries is through licensing regulations. As you may know, a great deal of academic research is published in journals, often owned by publishing companies or academic organizations. Many libraries, these days, do not purchase physical copies of academic journals (and many journals are no longer printed anyway); instead, libraries provide *access* to journals electronically.

The wording of that last phrase was very deliberate: libraries provide access. In general, most libraries do not own electronic journals; rather, libraries buy a license that provides access to their users. In this approach, copyright owners retain all of their rights and allow libraries to provide access. Often that access is limited in some way: it may be limited to a university's faculty and students, for example, or to a certain number of users at one time.

Although licensing electronic resources (including e-books) has been around for a number of years, it is a significant change from how libraries typically operate. Rather than buying material and owning it, now libraries are essentially getting temporary access to it.

Libraries have to negotiate contracts with the copyright owners (generally the publishers) to gain access and allow users to access the content. Because the publishers have all of the content, and it's very important to library users to gain access, libraries are at something of a disadvantage in these negotiations. Partially as a result of this, costs for electronic content have skyrocketed in the past decade; this has become known as the "serials crisis" because prices rise exponentially, while budgets remain flat or get reduced.

CREATIVE COMMONS

Given these issues with copyright, what should we do as a society? Some advocate for modifying the law and clarifying the fair use principle. Others, however, suggest that the current copyright law is too complicated and confusing; rather than making adjustments to this law, they suggest we find new alternatives.

One such alternative is called "Creative Commons" (CC; see https://creativecommons.org). This nonprofit organization explains that it "helps you legally share your knowledge and creativity to build a more equitable, accessible, and innovative world. We unlock the full potential of the internet to drive a new era of development, growth and productivity" (Creative Commons, n.d.b., para. 1).

CC offers alternative licenses to copyright. Under CC licenses, you can determine which rights you want to retain and which rights are unimportant to you. As CC explains:

> Those who want to make their work available to the public for limited kinds of uses while preserving their copyright may want to consider using CC licenses. Others who want to reserve all of their rights under copyright law should not use CC licenses. (Creative Commons, n.d.a., para. 4)

There are currently six different types of CC licenses, which can be explored on their website. These different licenses allow the creator of a work to retain some rights but not others. For example, under a CC-BY license, you would retain the right to have a work attributed to you but place no restrictions on how the work can be used, by whom, for what purpose, or anything like that. Under a CC-BY-NC license, you would retain the right to have a work attributed to you and to profit from the work, but you would allow any noncommercial usage of the work.

A final point about CC is worth making: these licenses are gaining in popularity. At the time of writing, over 1.4 billion pieces of creative work used CC licenses. Creators see this as a viable alternative to traditional conceptions of copyright, and it has been recognized as such in court.

CONCLUSION

In this chapter, we have reviewed the basics of copyright law and how it pertains to libraries. As this brief overview has demonstrated, copyright is quite complex. Many librarians opt to take additional training and learn more about it, particularly if their job duties encompass ILL or related duties where knowledge about copyright issues is paramount.

There are a few key points to remember regardless of how much training you have in copyright issues. First, the law has some specific provisions relevant to libraries and other information organizations. The first sale doctrine and the allowances for reproductions are important principles for libraries and archives.

Equally important, if not more so, is the fair use principle, which has four factors. These four factors should be carefully considered (and weighed equally) whenever you are trying to determine whether you need to get permission from a copyright owner for using his or her work or if your use should be considered fair use. The fair use principle is often particularly important in school and academic libraries.

Another important point with regard to copyright law is to remember that libraries want to avoid being legally liable for their patrons' actions. Thus, libraries should ensure that they have a copyright notice near photocopying and scanning equipment (the wording required by the law is as mentioned earlier). In addition, librarians can work with their patrons to help them stay within the fair use protected by the law.

Finally, we should remember that there are many facets to consider with copyright. If you recall the anecdote from the beginning of the chapter, a school librarian was looking for an e-book version of *Frankenstein* so a teacher could share it with her students. In this situation, for many books, you would want to consider the four fair use factors. This scenario would likely not be fair use because the teacher wanted to use the entire work and because it could have a negative impact on the market.

Before considering fair use, however, the school librarian should consider the publication date of *Frankenstein*. Because the book was published in the early 1800s, it is in the public domain. This means that it is not copyright protected any longer. In this case, the school librarian searched for the book on websites that host public domain books and found a version that the teacher could use for her students.

This example shows that copyright can be complex, but it is navigable. There are often other librarians willing to assist and share their perspectives, which can help determine the best (and most legally protected) actions.

NOTES

1. Copyright laws vary from nation to nation, despite attempts to create some reconciliation between them. Because of this, the current chapter focuses only on copyright in the United States. Specialized sources should be consulted to understand international copyright issues.

2. The part of the clause that addresses "inventors" is covered by patents, a separate area of law and policy from copyright. Most libraries do not have much dealing with patents, so they are not covered in this book.

REFERENCES

Copyright law of the United States, Title 17 (1976). Retrieved from https://www.copyright.gov/title17/

Copyright Office. (2015). *Orphan works and mass digitization.* Retrieved from https://copyright.gov/orphan/reports/orphan-works2015.pdf

Creative Commons. (n.d.a.). Frequently asked questions. Retrieved from https://creativecommons.org/faq/

Creative Commons. (n.d.b.). What we do. Retrieved from https://creativecommons.org/about/

Stanford University Libraries. Copyright and Fair Use Office. (2018). Library photocopying. Retrieved from https://fairuse.stanford.edu/overview/academic-and-educational-permissions/library-photocopying/

U.S. Constitution. Art. I, Section 8, Clause 8. Patent and copyright clause.

FOURTEEN

Intellectual Freedom Trends and Their Implications

As many people have warned, predicting the future is quite difficult and is likely to be wrong in some way (e.g., Vanderbilt, 2015). This chapter, then, doesn't attempt to predict the future of intellectual freedom. Instead, we review some ongoing trends related to intellectual freedom and consider their implications for the future.

There are some concerning trends when it comes to the future of intellectual freedom. Because of this, the future is uncertain and could be perilous. In response to these trends, we must continue to practice intellectual freedom in our libraries and other organizations. We will need to develop robust intellectual freedom habits and be able to articulate and defend the value of intellectual freedom.

TRENDS THAT CHALLENGE INTELLECTUAL FREEDOM

There are a number of trends that present challenges to intellectual freedom. Though some of these trends occur beyond the library doors, they still have the potential to impact information access in our lives and in our institutions. These trends threaten intellectual freedom in several ways, as the following sections describe.

Global Censorship

There are reports of censorship around the world. Countries such as China, Iran, and many of the Middle East nations routinely censor the information available to their citizens (Deibert, Palfrey, Rohozinski, & Zittrain, 2010). China is perhaps most well-known for its efforts in this regard (Shahbaz, 2018). It has a so-called Great Firewall that essentially prevents access to information about political unrest, banned religions, and other topics the government deems sensitive (Economy, 2018).

Freedom House (https://freedomhouse.org) monitors online freedom in sixty-five countries in an annual report. They explain,

> As we increasingly rely on the internet, it is important that the rights we enjoy offline are also protected online. The freedoms of speech, information, privacy, and association enshrined in international covenants are fundamental to the upholding of liberal democratic values. Even in closed societies, technology can penetrate longstanding political and media restrictions, carving out a limited space for freedom online. (2018, para. 7)

This explanation makes clear that online censorship occurring in other nations is relevant and potentially impactful in the United States. Nations study and adapt policies and structures that other nations use; if online censorship proves effective in some countries, its spread is likely to accelerate. In addition, repressive policies in one locale can affect freedoms in other locales, if a company decides to adopt a single policy across all locations. The 2018 report from Freedom House indicated that online freedom of speech has declined in 40 percent of the countries they studied. As we have learned throughout this book, any time censorship is in the picture, intellectual freedom is under threat.

The Right to Be Forgotten

This right has been established in European law since 2012. Essentially, a person has the right to request that certain information about their past be deindexed (essentially, delinked) from search engines. For example, a person may have committed crimes as a youth, which were published in an online newspaper.

As an adult, that person may claim a "right to be forgotten," meaning he or she wants stories about the youthful crimes to no longer come up in a search. Under European law, search engines must deindex such stories upon written request, provided it is reasonable. (Search engines may turn down requests under certain limited reasons, and there is an appeals process.) In 2018, Google reported it had received 650,000 requests related to this law in just four years (Doubek, 2018).

On one hand, we can see the value of such a right. People can change, and it may not seem fair to have one's past follow one around forever. Information posted online can last forever and harm one's reputation.

On the other hand, if information does not come up in a search about a person, it has effectively been censored. It would be all but impossible to find. One of the amazing things about the internet is the longevity of information once it has been posted—but the right to be forgotten is a direct challenge to that. The right to access information seems to be secondary to the right to be forgotten in Europe (Arthur, 2014). (At the current time, the United States shows no indication of adopting similar laws.)

Trigger or Content Warnings

Trigger warnings (or content warnings) have been increasingly common topics of discussion for the past several years (throughout the mid- to late 2010s). A trigger warning indicates that difficult or controversial content follows. It is a caution to those who may be "triggered" or experience emotional trauma or difficulty due to the content. Trigger warnings have been discussed in relation to college syllabi, for example. Imagine that a college literature course reads a book that includes a rape scene; should the professor include a trigger warning on the syllabi so that those who may be emotionally traumatized by reading the content can be prepared? One professor who applies trigger warnings wrote,

> The point is not to enable—let alone encourage—students to skip these readings or our subsequent class discussion. . . . Rather, it is to allow those who are sensitive to these subjects to prepare themselves for reading about them, and better manage their reactions. (Manne, 2015)

Some people suggest that trigger warnings are a way to be thoughtful and considerate of those who have experienced trauma. Others counter that trigger warnings are a form of coddling and disregard the strength of trauma survivors (e.g., Lukianoff & Haidt, 2015).

The American Association of University Professors (AAUP) cautions against trigger warnings, claiming that they impinge on academic freedom of speech. They explain, "The presumption that students need to be protected rather than challenged in a classroom is at once infantilizing and anti-intellectual" (2014, para. 3).

While the American Library Association (ALA) has not issued formal guidance on trigger warnings, the association is against labeling content, generally speaking. The ALA states,

> Prejudicial labels are designed to restrict access, based on a value judgment that the content, language, or themes of the resource, or the background or views of the creator(s) of the resource, render it inappropriate or offensive for all or certain groups of users. The prejudicial label is used to warn, discourage, or prohibit users or certain groups of users from accessing the resource. (2015, para. 4)

While trigger warnings are not necessarily intended to restrict access, they sometimes are used that way. Furthermore, to avoid having to decide whether to even use trigger warnings, some people are changing their syllabi, avoiding potentially controversial works altogether (Lukianoff & Haidt, 2015). This, too, has implications for intellectual freedom. Information that is withheld out of a fear of triggering someone is still information withheld. (For a detailed examination of all sides of the trigger warning debate, see *Trigger Warnings: History, Theory, Context*, edited by Emily J. M. Knox.)

Net Neutrality under Threat

Net neutrality is the concept that all traffic on the internet should be treated equally, regardless of its source. Under this principle, internet service providers (ISPs) should treat all data equally and not prioritize data from certain services, apps, or providers. However, this concept is under threat: many ISPs want to be able to throttle some data and prioritize other data.

For example, imagine your ISP had an arrangement with certain news media companies. When you searched online for news, stories from these companies would appear faster or load faster than stories from other media sources. The ISP would be prioritizing traffic from their partners over traffic from other sources.

This becomes important for a few reasons. First, it can affect one's behavior. In the abovementioned example, you might start preferring the media company whose stories load faster and disregarding other media companies. This could happen regardless of which media source is actually providing better news information.

Second, if net neutrality is abandoned, it will likely benefit companies with strong finances. Large multinational corporations could afford to partner with ISPs to prioritize their data, while small companies, local companies, and nonprofit institutions would be unable to do so. This would further skew the media and market landscapes.

Finley (2018) explains the connection between net neutrality and freedom of speech: "A handful of large telecommunications companies dominate the broadband market, which puts an enormous amount of power into their hands to suppress particular views or limit online speech to those who can pay the most" (para. 3).

This threatens the ability of libraries to provide access to a wide range of views and the ability of patrons to gain access to those views. It could have implications for less popular or less mainstream (or less profitable) perspectives.

Currently, the state of net neutrality is uncertain. While the federal government has rolled back protections for net neutrality, states and many organizations are trying to defend it through legislative and judicial means.

Platform Censorship

Platform censorship is a form of repression in which various media platforms restrict the circulation of particular views or statements. Often this occurs on social media platforms, such as Facebook, Pinterest, YouTube, Twitter, and Instagram. This form of censorship often starts as a well-intentioned approach, trying to reduce access to and the spread of, say, violent content or misinformation (such as anti-vaccine propaganda) (Cave, 2019). Platform censorship has been used to decrease the circulation of white supremacy content (e.g., Malcolm, Cohn, & O'Brien, 2017).

Corporations and businesses have the right to decide with whom they will do business and have the right to tweak algorithms and remove content that does not meet their terms of conduct. At the same time, many of the impulses that seem to motivate platform censorship seem benign or even positive—many of these companies are trying to reduce the spread of misinformation and harmful, hateful propaganda.

However, we must recognize that censorship is censorship. Free speech advocate Electronic Frontier Foundation (EFF) explains, "We must also recognize that on the internet, any tactic used now to silence neo-Nazis will soon be used against others, including people whose opinions we agree with" (Malcolm, Cohn, & O'Brien, 2017, para. 2). Some activists note that discussing racism on Facebook can get one banned for using "hate speech" (Guynn, 2019).

In addition, Breland (2019) explains that "on the internet, shutting down one community likely means that at least some of its members will easily go to another one that's often more extreme that the place they just left" (para. 13).

Platform censorship is a tool for reducing access to some forms of speech. It is a tool that can be misused and misapplied. As Malcolm, Cohn, and O'Brien (2017) note, it is too often deployed in response to headlines—in a reactionary manner. It also clouds the fact that "thousands of less visible decisions are made by companies with little oversight and transparency" (para. 6).

Complacency

The Children's Internet Protection Act (CIPA) went into effect in the United States in 2003 (see Chapter 10 for more discussion about internet filtering), meaning that many younger adults have grown up using filtered internet at school and in their libraries. They may also have experienced filtered internet at home (we have no reliable statistics about how many families filter their home internet).

Because of their experience with filters, many adults may be complacent about internet filtering. They may believe that it does more good than harm; they may see it as a positive way to keep minors from accessing controversial or dangerous information, despite evidence that filters do not work all that well—not to mention the lack of agreement about what should be considered controversial or dangerous.

Perhaps complacency alone is not enough to threaten intellectual freedom. Yet, combined with the challenges mentioned previously, it is not difficult to see that intellectual freedom in our libraries—and in our world—is threatened on many levels.

PRACTICING INTELLECTUAL FREEDOM

In the introduction, we discussed practicing intellectual freedom the way an athlete might practice a skill. Throughout the book, we've addressed many ways that we can practice intellectual freedom skills—such as how to handle materials challenges, develop and weed collections, and protect meeting rooms, exhibit spaces, and programming in libraries. We also discussed more complicated topics such as internet filtering, the #MeToo movement, fake news, and law enforcement in libraries.

These are complex areas, and most people do not easily master the skills to be proficient with intellectual freedom; it takes practice. What do we mean by practice? There are a few steps that can be helpful here.

First, rehearse in your own mind the steps you might take in scenarios involving intellectual freedom. If a patron challenges a book, what will you do? If a board member pushes for internet filtering, how will you respond? What if the state police demand circulation information about a particular movie? Thinking through these different scenarios and the steps you can take will help you to be mentally ready when challenges arise.

Second, ensure that your library's policies are up to date and tied into the guidance provided by the ALA. It is often helpful to include copies of the Library Bill of Rights, the Freedom to Read Statement, and other such documentation. Your collection development policy should list the guidelines for collecting and weeding. You should include a policy for materials challenges as well as guidelines for handling law enforcement requests.

Third, institute staff training in intellectual freedom. Use this book or guidance from the ALA to frame the training, and ensure that you are starting with the core values of librarianship. Hold role-playing games in which you take turns acting like patrons and staff members in these scenarios. Talk through the appropriate responses, and answer questions that arise. Let staff know what they should do when a situation arises.

These are all steps to practice intellectual freedom. Over time you can hone your intellectual freedom skills, just as athletes hone their skills. This will ensure that you are prepared when an intellectual freedom situation arises.

REFERENCES

American Association of University Professors. (2014). *On trigger warnings*. Retrieved from https://www.aaup.org/report/trigger-warnings

American Library Association. (2015). Labeling systems: An interpretation of the library bill of rights. Retrieved from http://www.ala.org/advocacy/intfreedom/librarybill/interpretation/labeling-systems. Document ID: 211cf21a-4164-b9e4-658b-35ef709f3e22.

Arthur, C. (2014). Explaining the "right to be forgotten"—the newest cultural shibboleth. *The Guardian*. Retrieved from https://www.theguardian.com/technology/2014/may/14/explainer-right-to-be-forgotten-the-newest-cultural-shibboleth

Breland, A. (2019). Why banning the toxic, racist 8chan message board could backfire. *Mother Jones*. Retrieved from https://www.motherjones.com/politics/2019/05/8chan-ban/

Cave, D. (2019). Countries want to ban 'weaponized' social media. What would that look like? *New York Times*. Retrieved from https://www.nytimes.com/2019/03/31/world/australia/countries-controlling-social-media.html

Deibert, R., Palfrey, J., Rohozinski, R., & Zittrain, J. (2010). *Access controlled: The shaping of power, rights, and rule in cyberspace*. Cambridge, MA: MIT Press.

Doubek, J. (2018). Google has received 650,000 "right to be forgotten" requests since 2014. NPR. Retrieved from https://www.npr.org/sections/thetwo-way/2018/02/28/589411543/google-received-650-000-right-to-be-forgotten-requests-since-2014

Economy, E.C. (2018). The Great Firewall of China: Xi Jinping's internet shutdown. *The Guardian*. Retrieved from https://www.theguardian.com/news/2018/jun/29/the-great-firewall-of-china-xi-jinpings-internet-shutdown

Finley, K. (2018). The Wired guide to net neutrality. Retrieved from https://www.wired.com/story/guide-net-neutrality/

Freedom House. (2018). *About freedom on the net*. Retrieved from https://freedomhouse.org/report-types/freedom-net

Guynn, J. (2019). Facebook while black: Users call it getting "Zucked," say talking about racism is censored as hate speech. *USA Today*. Retrieved from https://www.usatoday.com/story/news/2019/04/24/facebook-while-black-zucked-users-say-they-get-blocked-racism-discussion/2859593002/

Lukianoff, G., & Haidt, J. (2015). The coddling of the American mind. *The Atlantic*. Retrieved from https://www.theatlantic.com/magazine/archive/2015/09/the-coddling-of-the-american-mind/399356/

Malcolm, J., Cohn, C., & O'Brien, D. (2017). Fighting Neo-Nazis and the future of free expression. *Electronic Frontier Foundation*. Retrieved from https://www.eff.org/deeplinks/2017/08/fighting-neo-nazis-future-free-expression

Manne, K. (2015). Why I use trigger warnings. *New York Times.* Retrieved from https://www.nytimes.com/2015/09/20/opinion/sunday/why-i-use-trigger-warnings.html

Shahbaz, A. (2018). *Freedom on the net 2018: The rise of digital authoritarianism.* Freedom House. Retrieved from https://freedomhouse.org/report/freedom-net/freedom-net-2018/rise-digital-authoritarianism

Vanderbilt, T. (2015). Why futurism has a cultural blindspot. *Nautilus.* Retrieved from http://nautil.us/issue/28/2050/why-futurism-has-a-cultural-blindspot

Index

About the Author

SHANNON M. OLTMANN, PhD, is an associate professor in the School of Information Science at the University of Kentucky. She obtained her PhD in information science from Indiana University–Bloomington. Her research interests include censorship, intellectual freedom, information policy, public libraries, privacy, and qualitative research methods. Oltmann is the editor of the *Journal of Intellectual Freedom and Privacy* and is on the editorial board for *Library Quarterly*. She has presented her research at academic conferences such as the Information Ethics Roundtable, the Annual Conference of the Association for Information Science & Technology, the iConference, and the International Congress on Qualitative Inquiry. Her work has been published in the *Journal of the American Society for Information Science and Technology, Library Quarterly, Public Libraries Quarterly, Collection Management, Libri*, and *Library and Information Science Research*.